UNIVERSAL MONSTERS

UNIVERSAL MONSTERS

Bryan D. Dietrich

Word Press

Published by Word Press
P.O. Box 541106
Cincinnati, Ohio 45254-1106
www.word-press.com

ISBN: 9781933456911
LCCN: 2007940291

Poetry Editor: Kevin Walzer
Business Editor: Lori Jareo

ACKNOWLEDGMENTS

I would like to thank the journals in which the following poems have appeared:

Alaska Quarterly Review: "American Gothic," "Mars and Rumors of Mars"

American Literary Review: "In the Valley of the Kings," "The Monster"

Asimov's Science Fiction: "The Flying Dutchman"

Chelsea: "Atlantis"

Chokecherries: "B Movie," "The Oblong Box"

The Cimarron Review: "Monster Island," "The Slave Traders of Gor"

Dissections: "House of Frankenstein," "The Creature Walks Among Us," "Psycho," "The Monstrance"

The Distillery: "Budapest," "Delphi"

The Dominion Review: "Constantinople," "Venice"

Farrago's Wainscot: "Five Million Years to Earth," "When Worlds Collide"

The Laurel Review: "The Monster and the Gypsy," "The Monster and the Gypsy Moths," "The Monster Nodding," "Waiting on the Brass Band"

Magazine.Art: "Attack of the Fifty Foot Poem," "Mission Control"

Midwest Quarterly: "The Black Lagoon," "The Monster Contemplates Space"

The Nebraska Review: "Area 51," "Recovering Roswell," "Sasquatch"

Negative Capability: "Easter Island"

Nimrod: "A Sensible Longing"

Open City: "This Island Earth," "The Thing That Couldn't Die"

The Paris Review: "Loch Ness," "Skull Island"

Ploughshares: "The Projected Man"

Shenandoah: "The Bride of Frankenstein," "The Mummy's Hand"

Weird Tales: "Necronomicon"
Western Humanities Review: "*Ars Poetica,*" "Aviatrix,"
      "Maya Codex"
X-Connect: "Dementia 13," "Keep Watching the Skies,"
      "Lemurs in the Plumbing"
The Yale Review: "The Invisible Man," "It Came from
      Outer Space"
Zone 3: "The Birds," "The Eight Thousand Years
      Between Us"

I would also like to thank *Negative Capability* for
awarding "Easter Island" the Eve of St. Agnes Prize.

A huge fifty-foot thanks to 3D computer graphics artist
Steven Stahlberg for permitting me to use his digital
painting, "Psycho Girlfriend" (2005), for the cover. And
another to Heather Boyce-Broddle, graphic designer,
whose infinite patience and talent gave the cover both
mood and modesty, what all good monsters require.
Also to Paul Chauncey for the author photo.

Thanks to Marta Ferguson for her invaluable advice in
editing the final manuscript and for her support of these
poems during the years of darkness. Also to Mike
Arnzen, Bruce Bond, Scott Cairns, Harlan Ellison,
Albert Goldbarth, Veronica Hollinger, Richard Howard,
Steven King, Ursula K. Le Guin, Cynthia Macdonald,
Paul Mariani, Scott Simpkins, and Bill Trowbridge for
helping me keep the torches lit.

Special thanks to Hal Bowlin, Doug Bradley, Carolyn
and Jenny, Bill Coleman, Ross Dietrich, Matt Eck,
Nathan Filbert, Yula Flournoy, Stephen Frech, Lise
Goett, Count Gregor, Allen Harper, Tony Hays, Shirley
Hoenigman, Texas Jack, John Jenkinson, John Jones,
Kerry Jones, Andrea Krause, Cheri Larry, Darla Lee,
Jim Lewis, Karen Love, Marz, Judith McCune, John
McKenna, Beverly Micue, Heather Perkins, Rex

Perkins, Gail Pizzola, Tim Richardson, Duncan Rose, Vicky Santiesteban, Essie Sappenfield, Deb Seely, Curtis Shumaker, Sean Sturgeon, Terry Thompson, Uncle Troy, Chris Ward, Meg Wilson, Universal Studios, the Milton Center, that woman at Harry's with all her tiny shampoo bottles, and my adopted magical family who was there at the very end. Each of you took my hand as I walked with these particular zombies.

Finally, to that last, best universal bride, Fay Wray, whose dark groom came for her the year I finished this book.

For Mother
&
For Alice

CONTENTS

Missing Links

Luminous Bodies

American Gothic

*Do you have to open graves to find girls
to fall in love with?*
—Princess Anck-es-en-Amon
The Mummy

That body is not dead. It has never lived! *I
created it! I made it with my own hands from
bodies taken from graves, from the gallows—
anywhere!*
—Henry Frankenstein
Frankenstein

We belong dead.
—The Monster
The Bride of Frankenstein

B MOVIE

We both know if I showed you the monster
now, you wouldn't stick around, so let me
tell you first about the window you left
open, the long-handled axe still leaning
against the work bench in the shed. I'm not
above reminding you how very far
it is to the nearest hospital. You
chose this life in deeper wood, the slow
growth of honey mushroom over the time
lapsed canker-spread of citadels. I don't
doubt you still feel this a good trade. But then
the gargle in the vine behind the house....
The wheeze of your verandah's weak third step....
That growing knot in the air, your temple,
your stomach.... Too bad real life doesn't come
with danger music. We all have to live
with what silence we let survive between
our walls. Even now, as doom approaches
over your left shoulder, questions linger. Strange,
but if at this precise moment its mangled
odor caused you to turn, to witness the final
lunge, no part of that unexpected answer
could prepare you to be abandoned.

UNIVERSAL MONSTERS

*I've felt the weight of another head
inside of my head, leaning its skull
against my skull…*
                    —Albert Goldbarth

HOUSE OF FRANKENSTEIN

The father's fingers stroke bone, coax coronal
sutures into orbits. His movements, precise
as pulsars, tease each temporal process
into place. Inca, arch, crista galli…
all ache for what order his palms imply.
Bones among bones—but living, like scalded
bats—hands pick and cluck through plastic
carrion, a clutter of fake phosphates
that lie strewn across the kitchen table
before him. Instructions. Glue. An empty glass.

It's Christmas Eve. Hours only before dawn.
Quickly, each digit decides, parsing
parietal from palatine, cribriform
from cranium. Occipital, sphenoid (both
greater and lesser wings), canine, cuspid….
He must make sense of this. Find form. Already
he's sent his wife, the other children, packing.
None anal enough. None worthy to worry
what lies intentionally broken. This face,
features fractured, this human constellation.

Forehead cumulous, shoulders pitched forward,
his fingers fondle ligula, linger like love
along the mylohyoid groove. Order
above all, he thinks. Mental eminence,
then mandible. Mind, always, over matter.
Before his only son rises, comes to claim
this skull, the father knows he must make it
last, so much like the organic matrix it models
that, later, finding it at the foot of the tree,
the boy will see among its fifty-four parts
fifty-four more. The hand that made his own.

THE CREATURE WALKS AMONG US

First, the house lights dim. The uncertain scream
of a stage door stabbed open. Then the curtain.
A boy wanders in, the kind who reads Creepy
by owl nightlight. Letting sneakers linger, appalled
but complicit at the head's threshold, he follows
the sound, feels his way with hands flexed out before,
clumsy as a clubfoot mummy. The shower
shakes. A soapy scrim shoots back along its rod.
Now the skull, green as corpse gas, appears.
Hovering, gap-grinned, lip-lost. The hunt is on.

When, in the tall dark, my father would fade
into the flicker of bathroom fluorescents,
a bulge bigger than usual blistering
out under his shirt, I always knew what
came next. Father augury, fancy magic.
How many times—lusting after what, at seven,
I suppose I only half understood
of the grave—how many times did I ask,
"Daddy, do the skull thing," pray for him
to steal into my closet, remove that molded
tomb jockey from its case and chase me down?

Along the hall, braving blind turns, through rooms
tricked to treachery by sunlessness and sister
litter, it, he, would dog my heels, the skull
scraping tracer lines, designs, across the dark
the way tree-dwelling owls trail fungal phosphor.
Signs of our *own* night flight lingered only
in what places we'd left, while the skull, my skull,
my father's plastic mastery, haunted me still.
And ah, how I'd run, fretted to a fitful pitch,
tuned, twinned inside my head, shadowing
the shadows there, reflecting all—aglow
with terror and delight—I begged him for.

THE THING THAT COULDN'T DIE

Sunday. A car swerves hysterically into the oblivion
between tarmac and birch bark, a terrible black and white
terrain where collision never comes, only a rise in pitch,
a commercial, the last break before suspense becomes belief.

Rapt with the kind of kindergarten bloodlust only a fourth-grader
has had time to perfect, I watch from my dad's clutch, perched
on his Buddha paunch like a belly jewel while Count Gregor's *Creature*
Feature, this afternoon's TV terror, cackles eldritch and electric
from its source pulse, our ancient Quasar. Six embroidered owls watch
with us from the wall. I can hear Mother, off in her room behind the cloth
carnivores—one for each of us—getting ready to leave. My father,
sucking hard candy between his teeth, scobs my knob.
                                                    Back at the wreck,
the driver has lost her head, literally, the way her lover might
lop a rose hip. Her fiancé, mad doctor, et al., at last arrives,
come to collect her botched bouquet. He takes her head home in a box.
There, in a pan of secret goo, he keeps their love alive. At least
until she wakes. Mother, meanwhile, has made it into the kitchen
where I've crept on reconnaissance. Pretzels, pop…anything to fill the gap
between acts. Spelunking hamburger stew from the fridge, she says,
"You know that stuff's not real."
                                    When I return, the head has come to life.
Its eyes, reeling at first, resolving slowly into panic,
seek something familiar from their sockets, a body
of evidence against which to pit this circumstance. A backless
evening gown perhaps, a cameo choker, crimson pumps. Upstairs,
Dr. Dementia composes answers for the inevitable
end his love is just now waking to. His greater necromantic
lyrics—diagrams, flow charts, neo-Mayan codices that plot
the half-life of plasma—all suggest he'll need another corpse.

"Well, *you're* all gussied up," my father is saying. Mother, casserole
under one arm, beelines for the door. "Is that for the preacher?" Then,
"The dress too?" The head has learned to control things with its mind.

Mother swerves toward the TV. She stands for a moment between us
and our Sunday supplement. Possessing those with bodies, our heroine,
our fiancée-*cum-Brain That Wouldn't Die*, wages war. "How many
heads come back to life, really? This is sick," she says. I find myself
counting: *The Brain, Donovan's Brain, The Thing with Two Heads....* "You
have to flaunt it? Why can't we...." Trapped, the head wants revenge. People
die. She reaches for the off switch. My world shrinks to a single dot.
Daddy gets up, grabs for her. "Turn it back on." She pulls away.
Owls watch her fall. Her head. The hope chest.

Blood and Black Lace,
The Thing That Couldn't Die.... I remember them all. Lovers, madmen,
the thrill of possession. All of them, one question. Should you let her go?

THE PROJECTED MAN

I wander down rows of plastic magic—glowing
  The boy comes home to a house too full of
skulls and x-ray specs squeezed in next to sneeze dust
  decoupage and dead dreams, his mother nearly adrift
in genie bottles, fake ice where flies swim frozen,
  on the dhurrie beige couch, worn down with being
arrested, ruled by resin, still as the half-hacked hands
  worn, each hand beached on her belly like the dead
stacked nearby. I pass framed Charles Atlas ads, what
  things they are. She has been waiting on him
would have been pressed, once, into the end pages
  only to arrive, to reconnect, watch Dark Shadows
of *The Witching Hour*, maybe *House of Mystery*, all
  together. They haven't done this in years.
sandwiched between other promises. THINK OF THAT MAN,
  Waiting, what she's imagined has grown beyond
EVERYTHING YOU COULD BE. PUT ASIDE THE COMICS, GAGS,
  her son. Maybe the afternoon will spill over,
AND BECOME WHAT EVERY GIRL PANTS AFTER. God,
  she and the father rekindling what's become routine,
all the shit I remember.   Myself, I could never get past the magic,
  giving her a chance to forget the others,
even on my first "date." Then, now, what I think will impress
  the lovers
only mystifies. That novelty nickel, the hollow
  made of everything her life has ceased to be.
change I've brought to Debbie's today, makes my love
  The son. He knows nothing of this.
laugh, yes, but *swoon* is what I'm after.
  A girl named Laura has just become his
Madness, I know, but still I show her its profile, its single
  world, and today she'll be at her friend's.
side, the hole in the eye that, when squeezed,
  Asking only to go back out, he confronts
drenches the unsuspecting.

eyes that seem suddenly to collapse, frail stars
In this case, her.
    grown too vast. Gravity guides her nod.
Anger. Confusion. She grabs the magic
    Maybe wanting, what drives them both,
away from me. "Heads," she says—there is only
    what peddles a boy onto his bike, a mother into
heads—and tosses my mistake away. I swear
    her Monte Carlo, spins
away. It never comes down. So here I am still looking for
    her down the road, toward cities,
another one, another forever
    away from the plain and
hollow novelty
    out of their lives.
I can't forget.

THE MUMMY'S HAND

The poorest were cleared out simply, gutted
with a clyster, carted away after seventy days
in the natrum. Those with more means merited
syringe, cedar oil jabbed into abdomens the way
one once speared perch fresh from the Nile.

For these, the priests allowed their resin to wreak
sublime havoc. Stomach, lungs, the large intestine's mile
upon mile.... All forced by the body's sluice to seek
escape. Left now with so little, loved ones bore
away what remained, ricks of reticulated parchment, lime.

Those with the most kept it, jarred, contents torn
from flanks with Ethiopian stone. Stuffed with thyme,
cassia, bruised myrrh, brains removed by bronze tines,
the elite greeted eternity empty only of their minds.

He claimed, in the end, her rings would wear her
to the grave. She, you couldn't beat eternity
empty handed. But as they sat together, heavy
as those accumulated carats laid out before
them on the kitchen table, faces reflected

in facets—a cool trillion, grand marquise
alive with light, a princess or two blue as sea
swift, peach, pitted hearts, so many long-perfected
cuts—as they sat, my mother, possessed once more
by the jewels he'd once given her, asked, "Ross,

how do I get them back?" They remarried four
days later. But then, I don't suppose it's much about choice.
What tomb, which way we'll be embalmed, even whether....
Others pick which trinkets we get to take, diamonds or forever.

One seals her entrails in salt and alabaster,
god-headed vessels next to a copper ewer.
Another picks her trinkets, trades forever
for twenty dragonfly anklets, combed silver
inlaid with lapis, malachite, carnelian.

In the chamber of ages nothing is forsaken,
not even her bed, all gaud and gilt, her toiletries....
Here, they salvage everything, veils to vanity.
Golden manicure kits for the quick, the soul,
baboon-braced vases of unguents, kohl.

Soon, her son, hearing her tomb defiled, unaware
the body has been taken, will have the whole affair—
organs, headrests, chests, a chair inscribed Hetepheres—
borne, empty, to a place less molested. Giza. Eternity.

꧁ ꧂

Alchemy. What my mother made of marriage.
Once her rings were melted down, resurrected,
all evidence of exes consigned to some garage,
burned, emptied, she felt, I guess, less molested,
transformed, able to gaze again on eternity,

own her own new ring, its host of heavenly angles.
Each face, geometric grace, each diamond.... Well,
infinity. So when the first trillion—one of many
complicated triangles she so loved—came loose,
when the tube of Super Glue cracked, consumed

the recast cast of old lovers, old settings, old dues
long paid, she trudged back to where Peacock's loomed,
the original jewelers. There, with sonic picks and salt,
they found the right solution, reorganized her vault.

Seneferu, the father, Cheops, the son.
Throw in the mother, some seventeen million
tons of rock—enough, according to Napoleon,
to circle two-thirds of the Earth—and you
have a family foundering for solutions,

attempting to vault the sky. Egypt's blue
bloods knew little of irony, but there is no vault
without walls, no need for leaping unless
your world has drawn too close. Why else assault
heaven? Why arm against dust, must, the dead?

In the beginning was Nut, Seb and Shu. Goddess
of sky. God of earth. Rival suitor, air. Nut, head
over heels, spurned earth, her husband's dry embrace,
fell finally for air. Now she vaults all. Moon-mother, grace.

In first grade we were all given paper hearts,
told, each day, we'd get a red line for being
good. When our hearts grew full, our teacher said,
she'd let us take them home. I don't remember
topping off even one. Too busy with skirts

and skulls, I fell short. Terror, a love of vaults
and moons, smothering and grace, called me back,
turned my tidal learning. Dr. Strange, master of black
arts.... The dread Dormammu, ruler of cairns and cults....
Clea, dominatrix, creatrix, healer and sealer of hurts....

My dream was to *be* Strange, to fall for the tender,
tainted Clea, leap the pits of Limbo, and—almost dead,
one last finger clasp from the edge of Beyond, seeing
her see *me* filled with love—watch her turn. See how she departs.

Osiris. Last god on the left. One heart each.
Slap that sap-happy sump pump on the scales and step
right up. Take your position in the other breech
and let him guess the status of your soul. Imhotep
or bellhop, marquis or momma's boy, the bow

won't break if you balance. Body still crammed
with semen, phylum filler, love, watch the slow
gauge turn. See how it weights, separates the damned
from those just dreaming. He's an artist, this one,
and behind him, waiting, stands Amam, devourer,

eater of the dead. Up to this, the end, she's been
both head and heart, shackle and shine, mother
lode, religion. Her hand always on you, fitted
for your wrist. Feared, devout, simple. You, now, gutted.

THE INVISIBLE MAN

Lunatic, he enters the house, pours himself a drink.

He knows these empty sheets, the impression
another once left, the blood their first fumblings
tracked them with, how, later, she'd tack the same
over wainscot and window when he went TDY.

He unwinds himself, mad as May Day, vanishing by degree.

Her picture, actually the two of her, hangs nearby.
A trick photo. Double exposure. One head
cowed, clad in silver. The other wry, ringed
in red nimbus, needs he never understood.

Gauze gone, there's nothing left but laughter, quit clothes.

He wooed her first with flight, plied the air between
ground and guy wire each day just outside her school.
Whole air shows just for her. I'm told a chicken
farmer called the base once. Lost his flock to fear.

No rules now. He can do anything. No one left to blame.

After they married, the air shows escalated.
"Look, I'll make an earring appear. Diamonds,
designer dresses.... Nothing up my sleeve." Gold,
several hues, two hundred pairs of shoes, bankruptcy.

The world is his—houses, blouses, banks. Everything shines.

Butcher, baker, candlestick maker.... Doctor,
preacher, guitar lesson teacher.... He never knew
why she wandered. Coming back from long trips—
Japan, the Philippines—he always brought back treasure.

You can't stop what you can't see, and all he loves is blind.

Now he's here, sharing sheets with the one he almost
married, one who once fought Mother for him. Flashy
car, dashing pilot, two turtledoves.... One way home
from church. Between hairpullings they nearly wrecked.

His friends, his loved ones…. Useless as ties.

Later, the loser *would* wreck. Her husband killed, her own
life left fractured, features rebuilt.... She called the day
the divorce was final. I was washing clothes. Novella,
an old book reopened. Her son, quintessential bad boy.

But then, so much life…. So much of what we need…. He's chased.

His initials, TNT. Taught me to smoke. No, I'm not
making this up, but maybe it *was* her kid, the evil he feared
would rub off on me, maybe my mother hanging there,
part housewife, part Wasp Woman.... Maybe, maybe....

There are things one can't unsee. In the end, wounded, he tries to return,

See, it's their last day together, my father's final feint
toward redemption. He calls Novella, takes her
into the bedroom, pulls out his old ledgers, liens,
shows her how much he spent on Mother.

grows more and more distinct even as he fades, reclaims

"This," he says,

vein by vein a body, his, caught between hours, loss

"this is

become apparent.

lov

IT CAME FROM OUTER SPACE

Guess what, I'm not frigid! First words of the letter
I wasn't supposed to get. Then some bit about a new "fuck
buddy." She was forwarding my mail. Meant to be
apart only a little while. It's not as if we hadn't
experimented. Various fleshy pretzels had been tried.
But I was alone, there in the apartment with that
letter in my hand and a stack of bills I hadn't bled yet,
and I couldn't put it down, couldn't think what to do
except take it to the window with another envelope, begin
forging her name, faking the address so I could resend it
to the friend it was meant for. The sun shining through
the watermark, my hand butchering her Os, the light
making even my palms translucent, I swear I saw her,
my first wife *cum* second ex, through the pane, her skull
haloed in red froth, tendrils taking me back to every monster
movie I'd ever seen where the hero, haunted,
hunted, climbs the scaffold, mounts some stair, rushing up,
ever up with nowhere really to go, the unmanacled menace
close on his heels. Throbbing, cyclopean, hungry only
for his heart, it cudgels him free from whatever mooring
he might have once clung to, and here, instead, he finds himself
one small step from the balcony, face to face with that thing
he once wished would never stop, a single, horrible note
stuck in his throat. And the audience? Undulant, unsympathetic,
we stuff ourselves chock to the top with popcorn, we chuckle,
we cheer. But not for him.

THE BRIDE OF FRANKENSTEIN

I.

MARRY ME SOON. I mailed her the words
the week she left. Eleven scrambled
Scrabble tiles, language made shards,
tucked into a Manila envelope. Sample
syntagms, talk's tiniest seeds
stenciled brown on cheap wooden
squares. I couldn't know if in the mix she'd read
sorry mom or *mer-son*, *rosary* or *reason*.
Perhaps something less placable:
more masonry, *memory arson*.
She was a linguist, I thought, able
to parse it out. But nine thousand
miles, Australia…. Already too many trades bent
between us and all we might have meant.

II.

What *is* it we want when we want to be
married? Life? Word? John believed the beginning
began by word, a marriage of eternity
and absence where the universe, thinning
back toward singularity, breaks down
and meaning, infinite as God,
trembles. Particle and wave, eminence, throne.
Isn't that the irony, the power, of these odd
skulls we pack with exquisite imitations
of things—word, Word, marriage, monsters?
What isn't there, is. Each imperfect creation
risen from its gurney, seeking first cause, master....
It arrives in your room in the black night, late.
A face framed in gauze. It wants a mate.

THIS ISLAND EARTH

Atlantis. There must have been a few who didn't panic,
who stood atop the terminal moraines or, closer, the berm
crests waiting for rip currents to come. Watching the end
approach from beach cusp and spit, that last, vast synchronous
wave stippled and pocked with urn and amphoræ, a chair here,
an oil lamp there, whole walls of bull-leaping mosaics
prosaically unpuzzling themselves, the detritus of all
they'd built.... How they must have envied us our backward glance,
the lingering look that would long outlast their own, the return
we might make again and again to them, to this, another's loss.

*There are certain events so striking, they leave echoes
in history.* Some Titanic scholar said that. When I heard him
on NPR, I thought of Masada, nine hundred and sixty
human sheaths, how the Zealots beat Flavius' Tenth Legion
the same way eighty-two dazzled Davidians burned Waco
into our brains. And Roanoke, North Carolina. A whole
community gone AWOL: "5 foote from the ground in fayre
Capitall letters was grauen CROATOAN without any crosse
or signe of distresse." How about the Hindenburg? A tiny flash
behind a rear gondola and thirty-three dead. Or, that largest
of flashes, sixty thousand shed shadows in a city between
mountains. The people called it *genshi bakudan,* "original
child bomb." Cape Canaveral. Bad O-rings, seven dead.
Mecca. Bad air-conditioning, fourteen thousand pressed
to paved flesh in the tunnel between ka'aba and Mt. Arafat.
Lake Victoria. Biohazard. A million Rwandan bodies
floating like strange, blue fish. And on and on. We turn to these
the way one might worry a bad tooth, tongues grown blind, skulls
heavy as Zeus when his daughter sprang full grown from his brow.
Pallas Athena. Mentor of mind, woman of war,
architecture of sorrow. Poe knew her, knew how humanity
is itself a haunted palace, how ravens peck at the brain,
take residence over reason, how the rhythm of regret,
the burden of wanting to remember *having* wanted

is too like the raptor that waits for the weak, that circles the dead
with knowing. Even the owl—Athena's chosen, wisdom's child—
hangs, dark above dark, a silent presence above each field it sees
as pattern only: those who have passed, those too soon gone.
A poet, dead on his feet in a Baltimore tavern. A dog,
dust by a door in Pompeii. Even we who can't forget, tourists
in others' lives.... All suspect rapture is wrung from its root,
rape, from the sublime. Leda, Philomel, poor pagan King Edwin....
Each soul only a swallow between storms, a pallid bust, a door.
In Shibuya, a Tokyo train station, stands the statue of a dog, Hachiko.
Each day, for years after his owner died, he returned here, paws
crossed, ears cocked, waiting to fetch a master that wouldn't come.

Now, near the end, airport taxi idling, she and I stand, stones
beside a friend's cabin, Portland's salt wind hankering after
features that might as well be dead, her face already fathoms
from me. The pitch pine that groan above us seem green as sea
moss, mermaid's cups. For some reason I remember
her father's Waterhouse print. Seven naked sirens, a body
of water, a young man leaning toward it. Dizzy, I imagine her
this way, think of her standing at the edge of a city, scholar
of waves too swelled to stop for any sea wall. I watch temples crumble,
fires begin and, just as quickly, founder. Smoke, ruin, her last smile
swallowed up. Everything is island. Nagasaki, Nikumaroro, her,
the land of ash and orchis where she's headed.... The waters want it
all. When I stop swimming, she's left me. My wife. Hawaii.

PSYCHO

We all go a little mad sometimes.
—Norman Bates

If only there'd been no room at the inn,
no sheets to turn down, no shower to turn on.... If
only I'd missed that madness in her, the desire to be
apart, a private island.... Maybe if I'd met her before
I grew to understand Mother. Was the one
short life we spent together enough? No, eight

more, even a cat's senseless span, multifoliate,
miraculous, unperturbed, would have been
short something, inevitably incomplete, wan
in the way it must have been for Joseph,
his wife given up to a greater need. Spoken for.
Some lovers are always already taken. Tab B

pretucked, slot A unsliced. No *maybe*.
No *perhaps* pointed enough to perforate.
When I met her, she was sweet camphor,
fragrant, volatile, ready to dissipate. Imagine
a Wagnerian God. Now imagine you're deaf
to anything, any celestial yawp but that one

voice. You. Last priest, last acolyte of someone,
some *thing*, you can never hope to be,
become, belong to. Goddess. She. Aleph
and Tau, beginning and end. All that cannot sate.
That's the irony. The nature of desire. In
my mansion you'll find evidence. All I've done for

love. Here I've collected only that fear four
dimensions will allow. Really, it's what anyone
does, dissecting what preys, what must begin

with father and mother, albatross and owl, bird and bee.
We cut it open, clean that great yaw, saturate,
stuff, suture, set it striding again as if

form freed what it once was, that flawless, deft
creature we, seeking still to be awed, trembled before.
I've preserved everything. How we met, ate,
how I showed her my office, the room, #1,
where I first cried watching her undress. Baby.
That's what Mother still calls me. She knows my sin.

So, now, at the edge of the water, watching her slip away
letter by letter—NFB 418—I wonder that I dreamed it any different.
This swamp, this skull, this locked, sunk trunk.... All that gives us license.

CREATURE FEATURE

You'll need a corpse, your own or someone else's.
You'll need a certain distance; the less you care
about your corpse the better.
                              —Scott Cairns

THE MONSTER

If you wish to make a monster you must
begin with the most incommensurate
muscle, the heart, and following this vein
move outward, carefully, arterially,
as if each scapula, capillary, nerve
ending were, itself, your destination.

From the Haversian canals and crest
of Ilium to the islands of Reil
and Langerhans, from the ear's aqueducts
and vestibules, across the heart's isthmus,
to the last fissure of Rolando, you
will be guided by each cell's mother star.

Binding your bloody tissues like sheaves,
stuff them fitfully into that skin you
quilted harem-scarem during each dark
night full of doubt or, unaccountably, glee.
Steady. You must remember to keep your head
when, among the cast off limbs, you find it

hard to articulate your original
vision seen so briefly in, say, some tree,
its form lightning-tortured into life.
Work slowly. These fragments will not walk
away alone, nor, finally, will they grasp
the source of your indeterminacy.

Regardless of that one bone—cuneiform
perhaps, perhaps forgotten—you must believe
regret is your enemy. Take solace
in the work at hand, the hand that is
your work now. Insert tab A into slot B,
hoping each structure, straight or oblique, fits the spine.

THE MONSTER AND THE GYPSY

No one, least of all the monster himself,
expected he would fall for her. But night—
cast blue and green by the simpler magics
she knew so well—drew him into the circle
of her flame. She was a Gypsy, mostly,
motley and mysterious, cowled in a life
her hands had stitched together like her cloak.

And when he stumbled on her wagon, on her,
there in that thicket of poplars—so lithe
and smooth, dervishing in the dark—he could
not separate her body from the play
of light on wood. The cloak gave her away
though, and when, stiff, bandy-legged and frightened,
he came to stand before her—hands shaking,

stretched out, cupped, begging he thought for water,
for crusts, something from this warmth she half
controlled—she traced too carefully the life
lines of his wrists, his neck, the blue stitching
in his palms, cried. And, as he too let bright
water slip the ridges of each old wound
which bound him tight, she took him under her cloak

and into her wagon and played for him
a song that, like so many others, she
had piecemealed from the pine. He knew then, here
in the shadow of a castle he had once
called his wife, his womb, how masters can be
chosen, how shadows take you in, how songs,
Gypsies, monsters, all, are cobbled from desire.

THE MONSTER NODDING

Mostly, he could do no more than watch her
dream—this arch, that cheek, the instep of her back
turned toward him. And in the fire's timid
illumination, he would imagine
her naked, the moon's high sheen reflecting
from each small, elfin nipple as she moved
to a rhythm only she, the pale
chinaberries, and the long mute know.

But often, when *he* dreamed of how he knew
she would hold him—close, wet, both a bit blue
in the weak light—he feared she thought he would break
apart, unpiece himself at the seams.
His Gypsy would draw back then, hesitant,
imagining just whose heart he had
inherited from his master's vast puzzling,
whose grasp, whose penchant for eggs and broccoli.

And would he—he could see her wondering—
would he want to chain her as he himself
had been chained, had come to know the language
of whip, board, and bolt? Or would he count her
as he counted his beads, his poppy blossoms,
throwing the last away? Would he, innocent,
dumb, heave her into some strange body
of water, that womb from which he did not come?

Would he want to fork her with the lightning
he called friend, break her, stitch her into something
he could better recognize? The monster,
waking then from these dreams, cold and frightened
in a night too near this burning, would watch
the firm rise of her chest and draw from her
body a surer, more seamless breath.

THE GYPSY LETTERS

Bury me standing. I've been on my knees all my life.
—Romany proverb

I. Constantinople

Okay, maybe we weren't *made* for each other.
You could be right. And he probably *is*
too tall, a touch tender at the edges.
But then you never wanted me to smother,
did you? Aren't *you* the one who always says
the bigger the man, the lower his hedges?
He doesn't try to keep me or make me
over, doesn't expect so much I want
to scream—you know how bad the others have been.
And really, Mother, he's no more ugly
than I am plain. See, *he* doesn't think that.
Unlike *some*, if you know what I mean.

Sometimes I think I can almost see
what *you* saw in raising me. The apricot
tree you helped me plant on the bank of the Seine,
the look you took from what *I* must have
trembled with.... I can catch myself catching *him*,
just the same. We built birdhouses together
last week. Yes, birdhouses! Would you believe
it? White-pine castles to hang from trees, for when
we stop the wagon. And when we'd tethered
a few to our first ash, the most fetching laugh
chuckled out of him, and he smiled, and then,
Mother, then he wanted to dance. This monster
whom I've never called a monster to his face,
this man who seems so awkward, graced with grace
of other men, this fellow with a love of lightning, lace,
graveyard picnics—he wed me to his long mismatched embrace.

34

II. Budapest

And I wonder why you call me addle brained.
Still, this fiasco wasn't *just* my fault—
I let the monster drive the wagon. Okay,
maybe it wasn't smart, but I tend toward
credulity where love's involved. I'd strained
my back the day before, and the camphor salt
can make me punchy. The road to Vecsés
isn't too bad, so after the last ford—
its spring-bulged river behind us—I paused, reined
in the horses, and, as we came to a halt,
ponied up the driver's seat to Monster. Gay
and full of what life his master could afford

before the village burned them out, my love
took over, hitching those thongs to his chest
like new hands, like I'd given him his best,
last chance at being. He squealed. We drove
some while like this, me sleeping, when I guess
the road's rumbling woke me. Climbing from my cove
of blankets (some *you* made, Mother), from my stove-
warmed shallow into the light, I saw Budapest.
Budapest! God, was I pissed! But then, when
I looked in those teared, rare eyes—the blue one
first, then the brown—and saw there the sins
of his father, that old fear; when I'd undone
the reins from each furrow they cut in hands
still tremored, pieceworked, pained, I understood
what furies he'd fought in getting lost, the urge to prove he could
stay the raveling of threads, faults he knew as birthmark brands.

III. Delphi

I've been thinking about that fairy tale,
Mother. The one you told, with the maiden
who lost her hands. Some sorcerer wanted
her, bartered her from her father for a sum
of gold. You told me she escaped him, won
her freedom the first two times, flouted
this awful commerce by being clean as Eden,
by washing then crying clean her hands. Still,
I remember the man's return, his third,
how you said her father, sorry for his deed,
axed her free from fingers, palms, wrists—those places
where her worry went to breed. This, he did

to break up any contract, any word
which might have promised off his seed.
Later, after leaving hands and home—spaces
filled with nothing now—behind, she hid
herself in a wood, married a king who made
her *silver* hands, bore a child, and then,
just when she thought she'd put the pieces back
together, the sorcerer came again
to name her son a changeling, claim him sin.
And you want to know (you can be *so* black
and white, Mother) if the monster and I.... When
you might expect.... Are we going to wade
on in, plan for the future? Your tale didn't teach
this, though, to trade our grasp for another's reach.
My hands weren't given me by design.
Only now am I learning to use them, to climb.

IV. Venice

You've been dying to know, love, what it's like.
Well, Sis, dying doesn't do it justice.
Every night when Monster shambles in, comes
to me, stripped, his master's fine needlepoint stretched
tight, trembling to contain a love that's made him
large, I stare at him, hold him, clutch his length
of hair and claw him to me. It's my strength,
I think, the way I hold him down sometimes
that keeps him satisfied. And me? I've touched
every whole of him, made love to thumb,
toe, that buckled knee, tongued his bolts once or twice.
I've even taken *him*, invaded, piked

him, cradled and stroked his cloven head
as he does mine—goading, guiding it free
from hood and shade, this wood of creeping vine.
Do you remember when we were girls
together, massaging trees to ease their knots,
conjuring mud pies—a *whole man* once,
remember?—from the clay of the occasional
crypt behind the occasional church
we were told to steer clear of? And how arch
those games began? How messy the miracle
of shaping became? And then the chance
brushing of breast on breast, the tease, the hot
growth of those tough, tube-riddled, bloody pearls
building in our chests. Do you remember when
game turned earnest, and we tumbled finally
to earth? How we wrestled, always, with the dead?

THE MONSTER AND THE GYPSY MOTHS

She didn't understand at first why he chased them.
Why, at night, under the influence of blue wine
and moonlight, Welsh tobacco and surprising sex,
he crawled from their bed and ran naked to the forest,
into the space its thinning bristle began. Sudden,
revolting—like cold fingers bolting coffins, keen
to redeem some missing limb—the trees would claim
him as he whirled, lurching and skyclad, ponderous
and grave, veined strangely with pale branchings of scars.

She could forgive anything, this Gypsy, lover
of monsters, even the fact she would probably
outlive him, had already, any number of times.
She could forgive his massive ways, the constant
goofing that set her magic, so often, off balance.
She could forgive the looks and speculations
their pairing had accumulated. Such were the weights
that gathered to them. But sometimes, when he left her,
her pallet, her own body barely filling
the indention that remained, there in the candlelit
corners of their lanterned wagon, she could not forgive
this man, the child she would never bear herself.

She could not forgive him—when he was naked, playful,
blundering off on his own after the moon—
she could not forgive him his taste of independence.
But when, at last, she followed him to a hollow
tree where the night moths hived, when she confronted him
in the dewed half dark as he petted its brilliant bark,
the monster, trying to explain, stroked it once more,
watched a final moth return to its busy center
and turned to her. Then, he brushed her cheek.

THE MONSTER CONTEMPLATES SPACE

Of course he liked things big. It's why he loved
the sky. And when, under the penumbra
of some tree, he felt the accumulation
of years, the slow build of stone upon stone,
this edifice of scars he called a body
storing up season, the memories of the sun
on this toe, rain on an elbow, balm
on yet another forehead.... When he began
to account for the counting up of days
so recently spent out of context,
in other forms, other skins.... When he felt vast,

as if he were more than the sum of his parts,
as if he were large himself, larger
than mere fortress of shoulder, tower
of shadow.... When he lay there beneath
the separate leaves, experiencing
their pleasure, *his* pleasure at the patterns
their pieces made, diffusing but still
harvesting the light, he knew that he was
elm-old and that, like the planets the Gypsy
told him circled the sun, he was more
than just a collection of limbate rings.

Eyes closed, he could almost picture himself,
toes firmly planted in a field, arms
outstretched to that space lightning gave
the master his love from, and he could believe,
if only briefly, the wish to hold it all
was enough, that juggling those suns
in burnt hands—perhaps merely in mind's eye—
was almost *just* enough to make the pressure
ease, make his largeness seem, well, rational,
let him beat against the dark *between* the dark
and life's larger shackles, a ribcage rife with God.

THE MONSTRANCE

The glass people pictured there, pieced of fragment,
drew him that Candlemas to a low flame
not one of the windows *truly* contained—
rather, they only filtered the holy
light he found inside. There, in a filigree
of smoky amber, a priest's movements stained
the haze with dark trails of absence, laid claim
to each space his hands had been. Strange oddments
which the monster could not name lay strewn about
the altar, called him further, past the door
and into rows of straight-backed pews the faithful
had abandoned as night drew down.

The priest, blind but beloved by his town,
took the stranger who had come so late—papal
oddity that he was—in hand and lured
him to a small room where the monster's doubt
was comforted by a hole in the thin,
curtained wall. Here, just short of speech, tongued only
with motions, able grunts, with the blunt, lonely
mainstays of the mute, the monster named his sin.

Though they had found her, shaken, wet, a bit worse
for the river's wear, the girl the town had thought
drowned, that reluctant flower the monster taught
to swim, was safe now, sound. No lasting curse
would hang about his flattish head, no Hail
Marys need be said, no rosaries counted,
no incense burned. The monster rose, departed
his room, turned one last time at the altar rail
and balked at a stick there with a ball, a bell
at its end where it rested against the stones.
Inside it, the priest said, were holy bones,
then laid it in his hand, a silver frail.

LOST CONTINENTS

*The place they go towards is a place even less
imaginable to most of us than the city of happiness.
I cannot describe it at all. It is possible that it
does not exist.*
—Ursula K. LeGuin

SKULL ISLAND

I guess at last the wall became a kindness,
something, cut off as we were, we could stand
to believe in. Fourteen miles of thatch and thorn.
Blue bamboo thick as human thigh. No twelve men
could, shoulder stepping, see past it. What gaps
there were we pitched with tar, body lard, those
who would not listen. Reaching the other

bay, we stopped, pleased. It's not like we'd forgotten
the reason for such extravagance.
No. One doesn't set a seal on the world
without regret, but what had occupied us
so much those many seasons—the better part
of the island, what each of us knew lived
there—seemed safer having been cut away.

So when that pasty impostor arrived
from across the sea—that man in the *body*
of a man only—when he managed to come
between us and that which already stood
before our fear, when he claimed the beauty
of our loss for himself, I believe *he* saw
his acts as gracious, courageous, salvage.

Escaping past what barrier we'd erected,
driving hard into the interior,
he came at last upon the reason we had
all but given up giving up. So much larger
than any one of us, it was too like the wall
we fashioned: vast, insatiable, necessary.
In the end he brought out the beast we, ourselves,

had fed. Strange thing is, he failed to separate us
from our God. Even as he left with the source
of the fog that had concealed us so long,

packing it away to return, both bane
and breath, to a city so odd he had no name
for it but new, we understood, I think, how
nothing keeps your faith alive like providing

for its absence.

EASTER ISLAND

Once we had Gods enough to make a man
dizzy. Space enough. Time, to hank out
like rope from the hauhau tree. Toromiros
we had, palms that bled syrup, honey, wine.
Here, storm petral and prion vied with frigate,
shearwater and fulmar thickened the sky
with a bright porridge of wings. So we ate,
feasting on that little banquet of life
left us, stranded by the tide and fattened
on the too-forgiving bones of our dead
volcano home.
                    Still, Rapa Nui left us
lonely, and here, grown greedy for more
than this simple acre of God, we ached
to make our own, to bring Him, Them, back
to us across that watery divide. White
stone we slaved from Rano Raraku, red,
from Puna Pau. Six miles we hauled them,
our sleeping sentinels, stone wholly
divined for keeping watch. Nearly a thousand
when we were done, tall as six tall men,
tons and tons of them, gaunt, haunted, teething
the beaches like granite ghouls.
                                    Three centuries
of making, remaking ourselves, having
abandoned all that we had for what,
it turns out, we never wanted. Albatross,
porpoise…these no longer infected us
with what reverie they deserved. And the rest?
Once we had done with the trees, once the cutting
ceased, once we had used them up for leverage
against Gods oblivious to what we'd wrought
in their name, once we were left with nothing
but insects, a few chickens, that last temptation
of the flesh, we discovered we had found

only the least lesson of desire. Anyone
can empty heaven.

ATLANTIS

I have all but forgotten now what it was
       like. There was a time when I remembered
the way, the long rowing toward it, deep
       timbers in the earth flexing beneath all
I could see. The sea, what I knew of it,
       pitching me forward, back, now lofted, now
reprieved. Elation at every crest, darker
       tidings in the hollows. I shouldn't admit
this now, but I never owned a sextant, couldn't
       name the stars. Every journey outward
toward what awaited me was, well, luck.
       That was the glory of it I suppose,
the never knowing, the ever present
       likelihood of falling short. You see,
eventually the way stopped being
       a gift, old paths etched their windings
into me, mapped me the way lightning
       filigrees window glass, and I was left
clutching my oar in a lost land I found
       too familiar. Or maybe *it* found *me*
wanting. Regardless, I retraced my steps
       to the little coracle in which I'd come,
set my back to what land I already felt
       sinking, and attempted not so much
a return as another failure. If
       only, I thought, I could snag a landing
I was no longer sure of, some mysterious
       island with no discernible mooring,
afloat, submersible, vast. A last, missed kiss.
       Something. Everything. I've all but forgotten
now. Finally, now. Now that I've arrived.

AVIATRIX

As always, the hard part is believing
she's really gone, might never be coming
back, that somewhere between her last ascent
and the sea she found herself drifting.
Off course, veering from all she used
to love, she must have folded it in
on some island, a small place, quieter
than the hubbub back home, that vast madness
accompanying her unexpected
departure. Even now, there's no one,
really, to blame, no fallen one to finger
as culprit, instigator, saboteur.

They say she and the man she chose to flee
with might at long last have been found. Out
there somewhere is an atoll, Nikumaroro,
dry only three months every year.
Here, they say she *truly* left, unprepared
for how little we really leave. All that
remains is a Cat's Paw shoe, a box for flight
plans, a taste of the metal that took her
so far from home.
                    Answers though, no matter
whose, are far less luminous than the fact
of lack, the swollen deep. So when the wheels
of Poseidon rise at midnight, I let them
spin me back to her, to an image
of her still aloft, and there, caught on the cusp
of knowing and not, of understanding
and what must pass for glory in the face
of the ineffable, I choose my own
myth, leaving her brilliant and alone,
lost perhaps, but never overtaken by that
which washes us clean of even the temporary
islands.

THE FLYING DUTCHMAN

The seaworthiness of your craft has never been
the issue. Nor trim, nor mast, ballast or destination.
What tack you take, the uterine grit of sea foam,
each tern that haunts your wake hectoring after
scraps.... None of these alone matter. The question is
more one of undertaking. Why should you desire
to go? How many journeys have ended with never
coming home? The Mary Celeste was found, all hands
unaccounted for, adrift in its Sargasso bed
and rank with weeds, her hold barred against invasion.
John and Mary, the Rubicon, neither finished
their crossing. Abandoned. And then the missing.... Milton,
Ithaca, the Cyclops and Scorpion, the Sulphur
Queen. All of them lost like the Witchcraft, vanished
among legends that stretch out from Utnapishtim
to Noah to now. Why, you must ask yourself, bother?
When the General Arnold arrived at Plymouth harbor,
1776; when she found the dock ice-locked,
a Christmas blizzard beating the waves to plow blades, chains
too brittle even to weigh anchor, when the winds
harped through that sweat-soaked rigging like melancholy
ice wails and the men still caught in them froze there,
half notes, howling; when those left on deck found their feet
quick-rimed to wood and began, slowly, to lose themselves
among the strange, blue statuary they had become;
as the captain, untouched, moved from man to man,
sharing with them sparingly what few spirits were left
from a deerskin flask, praying only that their screams
would never reach the shore, you must believe he too
remembered the myth of the Dutchman forever
doomed to sail the sky, eternity unmoored, till love,
true and simple as a shoreline, were to tap
against his bow. You should believe this as well: no seaman
worth the salt he sails has asked for anything *but*
that, just that. Love, a death ship, and a star to sink her by.

LOCH NESS

Here, where the skeins have grown heavy with maybe
salmon at best, where even the choicest bait's gone
green—the strongest lines left snapped like string; here, where
charges dropped in the deep only rock the dark
water in its banks instead of setting spine
toward surface; here have I crept, combing
for a face among years of grotto waters. Still
I cannot fathom her. On some nights, when I skirt
the edges of this black loch, unpicked, tracking
her spoor between the lingering screams of blue
loons, I try to recall how first I stumbled
on obsession.
                    Don't ask me just how long
I've looked for signs of imminent return. Easy
enough to say it's sickness, that I've suffered
always a fascination with wanting
more than what the world names natural. Easier
still to blame this highland fissure, its suicide
plunge—450 feet, twice that in spots.
Maybe the murk of it, these sweet, subtle currents
prepared to purge a man with his own lack
of breath. Cold. Dismal. Doughty. Ambivalent
as a grave.
                    Here, in the sixth century,
St. Columba plucked another soul, a swimmer,
from her grasp, saying, *Think not to go further*,
touch not thou that man, unaware, perhaps,
of the man himself, what he may have wanted.
Did he fall? Or—mad already, only barely
treading this ghost-smoked foam between
shores, each wave's length obscuring having
from never having lost—was he pushed, consumed
with desire, gnawed by his own monstrous need
to be touched?

THE BLACK LAGOON

Living, he'd found, was about breathing. Deep
thought for a creature bare gill slits removed
from primordial ooze. But having left
the lagoon, that kelp-encrusted midge farm
he called home, having been drawn by love
out into a kind of relentless thin
air he didn't understand, all he could think
of was returning to the dark. Its, well, creature
comforts. So much more familiar than this
woman, her boat, these men with their barbed bouquets.

If it had been even a little different,
a rarer air perhaps, spear guns even
the least bit less habitual, if he could
have remained above with her or she below
with him.... But that would take another fish
story. No, he was born for the breaking
waves, something like Aquaman without the tights.
Okay, without his looks either. No kingdom,
no sea-bottom xanadu, no tank, no tidy
bowl. All he had on this side of the sea

was a lingering regret she could never
fathom. So, like the brine he needed
to survive, he left them both behind
and let the surgeons take him, remake him
in their image, reshape the porous
clay of lung and larynx so that he might shake
free, shuck the lagoon's dark swoon, clutch
a bit of botched life to what gills they'd left
broken in his chest, and wander at least
as long in this earth as the deep and its two

new faces would allow.

MAYA CODEX

These fragments I have shored against my ruins.
—T. S. Eliot

I.

The deep's green dream of jungle, itself a sea
of mangrove and chit palm, floats five thousand feet
below us. Cloud shadows like mad Mandelbrot
sets, inky islands cut adrift, surf a frayed
foam of banyan and botoncillo, crab walking
the peninsula the way great drifts of plankton
stain waves, carving cuneiform from Caribbean.

II.

Language. Forms. Mistaking one incarnation
for another. It is hard to tell these blues
apart. Sea. Sky. Her eyes in the right light.
Accumulated crystal pillars, piles of horizon's
breath frost.... Caught between these clouds and the Eagle
Nebula (Serpens, its vast gas columns grown
placental), only difference seems impossible.

III.

Chichén-Itzá in Mayan means *at the border
of the mouth. It is impossible to say
just what I mean.* Here, trapped on the forty-
fifth step of the Sun, fear-seized soles refusing
further ascent, I look out on five
centuries of neglect and wonder what pomp
preceded me. I've been constipated for days.

IV.

At the spring equinox it's said a serpent
descends these ninety-one stairs. Sol's shadow. God gone
to ground. As day wanes, the phenomenon
reverses—Quetzal returns to heaven, finished
once more with the world. It must have been glorious.
Priests, all robe and feather, snaking easily past
this place where, butt-first, humble, we gracelessly quit their temple.

V.

Dry land, dead crops, too many fucking people....
Always they ask for sacrifice. At the sinkhole
the priest provides a diver with what answers
he will need. *Memorize this*, he says. *Wait a day,*
return miraculously tomorrow and speak
the words. Then they push him in, run. No one,
they believe, should witness such hunger, harbor the holy.

VI.

The sun needs blood to render what has been
lost. Like us, it must travel the dark
places, tremble at the edge of forever
having fallen. No one knows what eats its flesh, what flays
its bones of light. But those whose hands we knot with vine,
whose hearts we hew for harvest—they know everything.
At least once. When what they've shouldered so long is lightened.

VII.

The film I saw said nothing of Itzamná,
the beginning, or Ix Chel, the coming, of Ah Puch,
handyman to this world's undercarriage. Rather

it doted on ancient astronauts, race
pollination, Atlantis, chiseled crystal skulls.
There are many mystic places in the earth.
Stories carved from stories transparent as our own.

VIII.

Always those in power keep their fancies
to themselves. At the observatory of Chichén-
Itzá, they hoarded all the best magic. Should the ruler
need new taxes, knowing the next eclipse seemed, well, prime.
So, from father to son, sky-scrying passed, leaving,
like now, the people to their darknesses, nebulae
not found in temple, nor astronomer's reflection.

IX.

Mammoth city ships—the Imagination,
H.M.S. Enchantment—float like ghosts into this
other world. It has never *not* been thus. Toltec
over Maya, Spanish over Aztec. But then
ideas conquer faster than people. On these walls
we find Mason and bodhisattva, Osiris, Ganesh....
Before corn, quartz, jade, we were made to trade in skulls.

X.

Itzabná. Son of God. Sacrificed. Quartered.
When his parts were finally gathered, the people
built four pyramids. Feet, hands, head. The best, they saved
for his heart. By the time the Spaniards came, only mounds
remained. They built a convent, El Corozon,
on the largest. Both host and guest to that algae
it breathes, they say coral can live a thousand years.

XI.

None of this is true, he says. *They pay me pretty
well to lie.* Our hobbled guide claims kinship with those
who saw the crucifixes come, the books begin
to burn. History, genealogy, tribute tallies....
Everything divine but their ruin. They kept
it all on fig bark, cured deerskin. When it was gone,
only the spines were spared. An impression. How they stood.

XII.

This is the second time through for us both.
Even on our honeymoon, there was residue,
palimpsest dressed in morpho menelaus wing-dust,
cobalt blue, like the eyes of another lover, veins
vaguely remembered at the tender of some sweetheart's
throat. A phrase, a gesture. I wonder at what brought us
here, love, this urge to assemble, so many ruins.

XIII.

Crested graun and iguana wander this field
where, once, twelve players in suits of stone courted
death, the first world cup. Between two goals they carried clubs,
a ball no bigger than a spleen. From that high place there,
obscured now by bromeliad, flowering fern, five hundred nobles
applauded the game. Perfect pitch, acoustics, making each
one twelve, they echoed a nation, multiplied themselves.

IN THE VALLEY OF THE KINGS

At the edge of all life, at this falling
away place where something deep stirs, brooding
heavy upon cliffs, its blue a bright cudgel
against stone grown softer than itself....
Here, where every magic I've never known yawns
beneath and, thumb by thumb, draws me down
to brain coral sprouting green as pili grass,
to sea slugs inching odd ochres over old lava....
Here, where Koko and Monoula overflowed,
slowed, formed from salt froth a birth chalice, this
blue bay I find myself sinking in....
At cove's tip, at the teeth of time's island
sanctuary, here, at the crush and crest
of a place waves christen Witches' Brew,
I rise on sea spray, hover among breakers
beating topaz into bruises more beautiful
than any sky they might mock, and think
of the Kino lau—spirits drawn back from flight,
back into flesh, back to this land of kō and kava
root, this grave cradle carved of bedrock and brine.
I think of the Kino lau, those haunted haints who reel
at the abysmal pull the world wields, and ponder
what wonder this rock-racked pocket of water plunder
must pretend so that they, the dead, our most missed
mysteries return, seduced from sea above to sea
below. I think on the Kino lau and understand
how, even here, I could only ever drown in her.

From the base looking up, only imagining
the climb, oblivious to that full mountain mile
that lay waiting, unaware of the stair, the nearly
three hundred steps I'd learn to love returning,
one foot set flat, the other already anxious
to test volcanic terrain, heart hungry to know
its own brim, never really having pumped
up another...could I have conjured any cup
half so full of words as this crater that's seen
a thousand years of silence, the mad, mute, odd
overflowing its crown? Through the early signs
of olonā, moa, sandalwood and wild yam,
up through monkey pod, mimosa, high dry bramble
and on finally to nothing but slate slab
and ancient lava roil, how could I have known
the dark tunnel still waiting, the sudden light
that would break like waves below, the spoor of war—
bunkers, pill boxes—lining the shoreward side,
all evidence that whatever once lay longing
to explode had since grown dumb? How unsee
the seen, this montage of old camouflage, shed
shells where so much life fell, bled, fed to a common
god, drawn to the yaw and tipped on in? No passion
pleads insanity, no climax without calamity.
There is, I suspect—standing on the cusp of this new,
old, bloody mountain, Leahi, Pele's dead sister—
no one I wouldn't sacrifice to find her waiting.

Up through abattoirs of uneven green
I duck the clutch and catch of vine, of maile
spine, what remains of veins fetched down as if the air
itself expressed desire to descend, incarnate
in Wao, the forest, these wooded ways. Light
licks the shanks of the hau, koa and kauila,
barters dark from the bark of the māmaki,
lingers in iliahi fingers, grows fond, touches
an unfurled frond as if it understood the wood's
long lust, this language of root, rock, loam, dust.
Moving between greens—the glow that makes
ironmongery of each ulu leaf, each reach
etched earth artery—I suddenly shoot free
from cane canopy, this panoply of yellow
kalo and emerge, face to face with stone.
In an iridescent crescent the cataract comes
down, a thin shim and hiss, mountain mother piss
arcing off an endless wall down, down through this.
Moss, dross of ages hangs heavy behind the flow,
patterns shift and suppurate into grotto,
what lies below, and form a pool where slag-stacked
rocks have gathered in nooks, generations of stone
collected like books or spurs on bone, caressed,
dressed, left here for gods, the Menehune, trolls.
Counting ti-leaf-wrapped tolls, these love loaves
that litter foot and font, I sit, wonder, *what do I want,*
wade in, curl up, and leave my luck for her.

Under an arcane arch I wander lost
among the transplanted, culture-crossed,
into Honolulu Museum's Mystery
of the Nile. Through aisles of urn and artifact,
lines that unwind like Hatshepsut's bawdy burial
linen, each surface inked in kohled ruin, I trace
a race's dread, the warp and weft of all that's left,
one more closed book. Of the dead, I know
little—charms, spells, turquoise bells woven
into brittle wraps, long-murdered maps of a world
five thousand years unfurled—but of the living, even less.
Chinese, Japanese, Polynesian, Thai—these faces
that pass between crest and chest, Isis and Horus,
Osiris, Bes—even these seem pressed from the past
buried in a valley of kings. Līloa, 'Umi,
Kamehameha…. Hawaii, Havaiki,
Ra 'iātea…. So many names, leaders, led.
So many cities of the dead. Heaven built
on graveyards. I'd never guessed. But even Bast,
Sekhmet's second sister understood how wood,
water, town, sod grow fast over the last
best incarnation of god. In Egypt, Nut swallowed
the sun to give Earth its birth each next day,
and Bast herself (first lion, later cat) chose burial
by the thousands in coffins of bronze and papier
mâché. Cat mummies cradled in cat-shaped clay.
Islands within islands. I imagine her in me this way.

MONSTER ISLAND

I.

Her hands worm busily down the waist
band of white cotton briefs, two fingers,
livid and trembling, driving the known
from her body. Hips rise to meet the slight
curve of each digit as ridge and whorl replace
me in the dark upstairs. Downstairs, I come

to believe my own palm the only answer
to what space still separates the darknesses
between us. I have grown accustomed to this
tidier world, this fantasy—glossy
waifs, paste-paper panty boys to torture,
a penis blind to what I fear won't wait

for me in the bed above. Tomorrow
we will sit in silence, each imagining
the worst. She will see me having stolen her
life, I, her leaving mine. Both will think things,
terrible things, and those thoughts will have form
and void, and from them all matter of beasts

will arise. New life. New death. We have reached
this midpoint somewhat less *together* than planned.
And though *apart* doesn't quite capture
the conundrum either, neither wants to
recall having once walked the house in tandem
shutting doors, locking cabinets, setting free

the monsters.

II.

It's easier at the movies, in that species
of dark where so much more is forgiven.
1969. My father takes me to see *Destroy
All Monsters*, a glorious Japanese film
failure, and together we overlook
Mothra's guy wires, Godzilla's glaring

zipper, the way so many lips always seem
to fumble, allowing only the just
wrong words to slip away. It is here—
147° East
longitude, a great deal less latitude,
north somewhere, the Pacific theater

perhaps, near Tokyo on an island
of pumice, shale, shrike, a millennia
of dead, spineless water gods—here, in *this* dark,
the monsters survive: Rodan, Aspiga
the spider, Manda who leveled London,
Anzilla, Bosaurus, other lesser infamies.

This is where they go when they're done
being difficult, though none are ever *really*
finished. Always we need something larger
than us to help halt the typhoon, deflect
the Kilaak transit beam, fight yet another freak.
And so this island. A place of rest. So monsters.

For the future.

MISSING LINKS

Up here it's neither moon nor earth.
Tears freeze.
Oh Yeti, semi-moonman,
turn back, think again!
                    —Wisława Szymborska

NECRONOMICON

First, feel the itch. It will begin like sin,
a growing glass glissando down your bones.
Next, wander your halls, a haint haunting familiar
rubble, this embarrassing stubble stumble
of standing stones. Ignore doors, swelling floors,
seek the catacombs. Now, find your enclave,
your cave, that library you've lined in shadows
from the grave. Dead words only alive
as long as eyes allow, as long as lips
crave. Next, peruse the staggering stacks,
reach for what attacks your fancy and draw
it down. Fear the possibility you find
there, yes, but notice the embossing, the gentle
spindles of what once might have been
thorns, now simple *f*s and *p*s, never enough
*e*s. Fondle the spine, feel how it breaks
in the space where leather meets leather.
Lover, tether. Listen. Can you smell it?
History. Remember that it cannot *not*
contain that place where you will end. Imagine,
though, what might ensue. Take the risk. Do.
Tell. Open the book, brace yourself, say the spell.

DEMENTIA 13

I meet a woman, a worker of words
who loves O'Connor and Hitchcock's *Birds*,
all horror stories, the better for worse.
She's gay and Wiccan, a comely curse.

> *Zombie, chainsaw, fetus, hook,*
> *athame, candle, bell, book.*

Her spell is modern, her interests, mine.
She knows of Triffids and Cepheids and Sime.
She, too, once sat in the glow of the screen
while the monsters processed and summer grew green.

> *Alien egg sac, mouthful of brains,*
> *priest on the sidewalk, count the stains.*

She takes me first by neck, by eye,
then takes me again with the gorgeous lie
of language spun from the life she's not
lived so much as faced and fought.

> *Tooth, claw, razor, bone,*
> Halloween, Twilight Zone.

The monsters she has staked and boxed,
buried out by the hollyhocks,
outnumber mine by kith and kind.
Hulk, brute.... Malign design.

> Rosemary's Baby, Eraserhead,
> Race with the Devil, Dawn of the Dead.

I want her to know that I understand,
that sometimes the thing in the dark, The Hand,
is still attached to a heart that speaks.
The first date comes. I rent her *Freaks*.

Stalker, slaughter, barker, blight.
We live and love in black and white.

A SENSIBLE LONGING

...to the empty trapeze of your flesh,
O Magdalene, each comes back to die alone.
Then you, the burlesque of our lust—and faith,
Lug us back lifeward—bone by infant bone.
                    —Hart Crane

I.

At six, everything is lightning. All you say, all
you see. So when the sitter told me we weren't these
bodies seeing, rather, extrusions of God,
some *else* inside peering out, even then as we sat
in her window seat watching the storm come,
I wondered how she, so old, could hold eternity.

II.

They had to break his legs to close the coffin, this man
who ran a bull to ground at sixty, survived lightning,
lymphoma, life. Son of the son of a king's daughter.
Each night he anointed his knees with WD-40.
Sitting on the bed, huddled over his arthritis, my grandfather
looked like he would when he died, fetal from neglect.

III.

When I was seven I wanted to believe in monsters,
wanted to *be* one, perhaps to explain why I felt,
already, so alone, like the figure in that resin
model I'd have killed for: *The Forgotten Prisoner.*
All bones, rags, chains. How many nights did I bind
myself to the bed, those dreams, inventing voices of rescue?

IV.

My youngest sister woke one morning with a lump
on the back of her hand. My first wife found three,
over the years, in her breasts. My dad, one along
a steep stair of spine, dug it clean with a potato knife.
My mother, another sister? Both had to have twins, old
body fossils, removed. So much skin. So many reasons to cut.

V.

When they took her in for the operation, my aunt's doctors
found more than what they'd bargained for. Half a century
into her life—having seen two sons grown large enough
to lift Volkswagens, take on twenty Choctaw at a turn,
burn through steroids and the CFL only to hijack
a haul of Cub Scout Christmas trees—she named the tumor Misty.

VI.

A trailer park in town offers the white trash dream:
Breast implants, FREE with your purchase of one double-
wide, duotone mobile home. Then there's that Canadian
performance artist. Has plastic surgery done for art,
films each operation. Breasts added to forehead, labia
to her cheeks. Horns, hymen, performance, pain. All opera.

VII.

Everyone wants out. That's the deal we cut coming in.
Each reach reminds us just how much the skin can't touch.
The plantar's wart they pulled from my sole like a plug,
the cysts my sisters insist augur bad blood, feet (Walker
feet they call them) overswelling their shoes.... None of us
fit our fur, slim slippers left behind. So we sit. Pass the knife.

VIII.

Finding my reflection in mammoth mammaries,
mud-flap mirror women who swallow highways whole....
Letting my siblings dress me, a pederast's dream geisha,
penis grown hard inside sister silk.... Two marriages,
two bisexuals.... When have I *not* been betrayed by skin,
transgressed flesh? My ass, even *it* gets wet when I cum.

IX.

In the Dominican Republic they call them *guevedoces*,
eggs (or testes) at twelve. All those boys who haven't
developed, ambiguous, raised as girls till the body
condescends. Here, we make them scarecrows, little gods. Take
that one kid—the good, gay Shepard lashed to a line fence outside
Laramie—did he forgive how they used him to escape?

X.

It's not that I *want* to be woman. Does a woman
choose not to close her sex, set seal to that sea
source as she passes, herself, through the unsettling
saturation of another? No. Nor do I hate men.
It's just, I don't *get* guys, can't talk cars, and *being*
male, lesbian perhaps.... Who do I have to fuck to be free?

XI.

Marz was my first. Back row. Nine-o'clock screening of *Bambi*.
Later, there was Janna. Bucket seats, VW, Mentholatum.
One wanted to be David Bowie, the other, Bovary.
Neither held a candle to Mary, she of two voices,
two lives, all false. And what about Chris, when he and I locked beards,
gave up? Or the woman who always screamed *No*, to get off?

XII.

Lately I have to wonder what it's worth. Woman
and man, woman and woman, man and whatever
leaps along. The trouble with sex is its simplicity.
Same reason I can't write eros. Nothing to say. Oh, we wish
it more than chemistry, blood. Beast must or bust. The real irony
lies in seeking, for the sake of flesh, only how to shed it.

XIII.

A nurse I know says Jamie Lee Curtis was born a man,
well, close enough. Triple-chromosomed, XXY. It's why
she has biscuits for abs. One in twenty-five women
sport two vaginas. Iguanas, two penises. Fleas are hung
like bucks, but braided. And female hyenas, they mount their males
from behind, clits grown large, impervious to reason.

XIV.

Sex, death, mound, lump. The things that come between us.
My wife and I defy desire. She? Motorcycle mamas.
Me? Nancy boys. Woodworking would be her. Poetry? Guess.
Romance, for her, means mind. Myself, I'd ask a rose.
And so we row, pulling forever against our own
best selves, mountain and whirlpool, plugging and unplugged.

XV.

Lot's wife looked back, longing, on all that buggery.
Orpheus peeked, punishing his bride. Even Inanna
strode naked into hell, jonesing for her sister's sex. Salt,
loss, crucifixion.... No price too high for return, grave cave,
what calls. In Laetoli, Tanzania, three sets of pre-
human prints flee across ash. One turns tail, back toward fire.

XVI.

Where my nightmares fall, the living dead follow.
It's always the same: I'm alone. Some strange city. Night.
They come from the dark, out alleys, the gutted bellies
of derelict cars, dropping crumbs of themselves as they go.
They crave only me, what life they scent lapping my ribs.
If caught, I become. One bite. I wake to want, their sleep.

XVII.

The night my uncle told us how to kill a zombie
we lay packed like corpses into my aunt's drawing room.
Six abreast, my sisters, cousins, and I watched the Mushroom
People come. Late night horror, double feature. Something
strange in the water. The crew changes. The ship sails on.
Pour in salt, he said, *sew the lips shut. Only.... You must get close enough.*

XVIII.

One cousin died of a cave-in, his brother of AIDS, their parents
from two-in-a-million diseases, Gehrig's and Beret's
respectively. Same year, my other grandfather. Gangrene.
And his sons. Diabetes. Eyes first, then legs. One aunt can't find her bones.
Actually, I suppose, it grows on you, spelunking the skin
like cave fungus. The family tree. Dutch elm. One limb at a time.

XIX.

I guess I should've known, since he wore diapers at ten.
But I was thirteen before I understood his blood
was killing him, my cousin. Taught me penises. Gave me hand-
me-downs, bell bottoms, and, later, Izods which I deconstructed,
thinking the gators too cute. He bequeathed me an old monster
shirt just before some quack took his legs. Paisley, piecemeal, all seams.

XX.

It's all about seams. How we fit ourselves, each other.
Family, lovers, what humps we share climbing down the eaves.
All the way down, to the cellular, the subatomic. *Parts*
is parts, says one commercial. *People is people, is potatoes,*
is dancing. Even muppets exchange extremities. ACGT.
JHVH. 4 x 4 x 4. Sixty-four letters in the name of god.

XXI.

As a child I crossed a creek with a broken arm, fell
in, got beat. My father never understood the ineffable.
Once, even younger, playing with a board, I clipped a girl
across her chest. The teacher raised my victim's shirt, made me see
my first breasts. Too like the dead of summer, when my cousins
built that haunted house. One handed me an eyeball in the dark.

XXII.

Patton teased transcendence from the souls he sent packing,
believing, as War, he'd suffered the same. An old soldier, it was his
halberd that clove helms for Christ in Caesarea, his hand
on the spear that split Galilee, on the knife that made
of Caesar a sheath. Before that, clamping closed each adamantine
manacle at Caucasus, his cheek grazing Promethean thigh.

XXIII.

For each of us the doorway's different. I've been looking
since Tolkien took me, since Lewis unmade my wardrobe's
sad mundanity. I remember crawling in, closing the door,
praying it wouldn't open on Oklahoma, again.
Later, in Memphis, I wandered the forest's uncanny
green each day, arms out, eyes up, beckoning the bosom of Barsoom.

XXIV.

Uncle Kenneth and his son left this life on nearly the same day.
The former chose an ex-con, a car hood for catharsis, traded
sentience for a stolen six-pack. In the hospital, waiting
for some purpose to unplug, I read about Howard Hughes, how *he* danced
off in a diaper, tissue tins for taps. Ken Jr. just vanished.
We found his Honda at the airport. Three years, four fingers of dust.

XXV.

Milton meeting Galileo, both blind.... Mingus and Bobby
Fischer swapping pawns in Bellevue.... Crowley cuckolding Yeats
with a kitchen knife.... I've rarely met *my* other, had nerve
to observe the observer, see how I see. Everything,
all of it revolving, the center, me. Since I was fourteen
I've tested twisted trees, each birch archway, for ways to flee.

XXVI.

Aunt Joyce lived her life pretending purple passed for pretty,
imagined, I guess, it accented her arms. Once, her daughter's
dress caught in a car door. She drug her two blocks before stopping.
Once, she waited three weeks to call the cops, her gun-wagging ex
run off to Reno with the kids. What, I wonder, did she see when she stopped
seeing, the world whirled closed, her last crash collapsed the light?

XXVII.

My friends—condemned writers all—swallow their sentences whole.
One believes in Bigfoot, another, that light lifted
him, lit his longing from within, let him live. Still another
claims AT&T can kill through the phone. The one who hails
from Cuba thinks her own novel a threat. It's about werewolves,
fucking, faith, the fictions that feed her female lead's descent.

XXVIII.

Tim says he was reared by Southern Baptists. Apt. Me too.
For years, caught between dreams of the dead and rising again,
I ran nuclear newsreels, apocalyptic loops, through my head,
craving, I suppose, carrion comfort. Lately, in the news,
another baby wearing a *What Would Jesus Do?* bracelet
turned up dead. Lead poison. The dangers of heavy metal.

XXIX.

I still consider Christ. Not theirs. Mine. Door to another order
of existence. Struck, stripped, penetrated. Pegged watershed
of blood. Unclean mendicant, eternal menstruant. Opening
through which each child must pass. Tomb, maybe even womb
weary. Side split, saltwater spent. Sent sacrifice. Gene splice.
What we cannot bear. Ear to the belly of the world.

XXX.

A man stands behind the camera. Before him
a twelve-foot ape climbs the side of an orphanage.
Flames frame our hero's fur, cornices collapse, monkey
and moppets survive. The man—Ernest Schoedsack, war
wounded, blind, best known as architect of another addled ape,
fifty feet plus Fokkers—calls *Cut,* bestills the beast in shadows.

XXXI.

They call her autistic, high function, dither over devices
she's designed. One cradles her, pressing in all around. Hugging,
she's found, settles her skin, allows her to tinker with other toys.
Taint. Talent. Inward turn. All sacred, all space. How she survives.
Humane slaughterhouses are hers. Kill chutes spiraling down like DNA.
She says she sees through *their* eyes. That way, they can't see it coming.

XXXII.

A man stands beside a fire beside a lake. Dragging
his bum foot behind him, he approaches the flame.
His best friend, brother, sometimes lover, lies drowned
on the bier, once-lazy locks licked clean, arrested in ash.
Ribs blacken, grow slack, crack. The poet thrusts in his hand,
hauls the heart out whole. Always the last to burn.

XXXIII.

How long, our coattail of cadaver. How brash,
the ways we wear this corpse. Forgetting, sometimes,
to covet the way we should, we lose our sensible
longing. But when she touched my lump, diagnosed
the bump (sebaceous something or other), the doctor said,
"The body can surprise you. Pay attention."

(1965-1998)

THE INCREDIBLE SHRINKING MAN

I was loathe at first to recognize it,
the slow increments of diminution,
how the world continued in its insistence
to grow vast. Suits become sackcloth, bones
febrile reeds, simple kitchen cabinets
more and more inopportune. Evening
ablutions—gargling say, or flossing—all
blown large. All of it a chore. Everything,
even my wedding ring, seemed to swallow
me. But then I'd never imagined how
beautiful it could be to touch the surprising

curves of black locust blossoms from *inside*,
to clutch such clappers of a tree's cathedral
bells to my chest or ride their pollen back
down to the ground, to make a modest meal
and sit, feet swinging, amongst the petals
of hoary puccoons, jacks-in-the-pulpit,
to count the molecular cracks in skarn,
imagine gnosis in gneiss, carve caves
for myself in alkaline feldspar or saddle
a saturnid moth for moonlight dragonfly
drag races, each libellulid left in the dust.

Yet all of this, my final rush, crush, collapse
came only after the truly exceptional
stages, those that offered up more disruption
precisely because they were less. Obscure
moments, really.... Noticing, for instance,
my wife's aureole, each new crude colony
of hair, perhaps the crow cracks murdering
my mother's eyes, or simply the nameplate
above my office door. Each manageable, lush,
lovely thing had telescoped just enough
to make me wonder. Was I still interesting

as I once imagined? Or had I grown too little
astonished with this plane?

ATTACK OF THE FIFTY FOOT POEM

This just in. What eye-witnesses had claimed
to be a giant villanelle roaming
the rural Kansas wasteland now appears
to be a pantoum gone aubade. Sources
speculate it may be poorly behead
ed, perhaps a case of truncated metaphor.

We should note that experts *are* at the scene
now and assure us, once the rampaging
verse settles down, their attempts at scansion
will be more precise. Meanwhile, a local,
Maya Angelou, has offered to pen
a dozen or so inaugural lines

in a last ditch effort to cap this terror
and drive it to ground. Officials, unsure
how volatile such a combination
might be, have, nonetheless, thanked Angelou
for her inspiration. Damages,
estimated so far in the millions,

are escalating. As we speak, the meter
is still running. Authorities seem averse
to bringing in the heavy artillery.
Something about no justification
for *deus ex machina*. One unnamed
serviceman blamed, quote, "blooming anxiety,"

while others have cited studies on "coda-
pendency," the need for *some* sort of crisis.
While in the flatlands there may be no cliffs
off of which to run the beast, many still
wonder if we're reading too much into this
threat. Further updates as news from the front line

breaks.

LEMURS IN THE PLUMBING

I have to wonder why I'm not more
        surprised at this, the latest intrusion.
It's not as if I'd been expecting
        relatives to swing by, but going
down to the basement felt like coming
        home, all pounce and prehensile madness.
They must've been there for quite a while,
        hooting it up, brachiating
like long-limbed laurels—hardy, hungry,
        full of dark and Darwin. Their fingerprints
stucco the nickel plating like whorled dimes,
        and banana peels, funky with silt,
saliva, age, drape from each elbow joint.

        This is why I haven't been able
to take a bath in days, why I've grown
        fragrant, unkempt, wild. I keep finding
strange leavings in the drain. Hairballs, steaming
        monkey business. Everything below—the waste,
what crap we've amassed in vast domestic
        intestines—has turned to jungle. Worse,
every time I descend, I can't help but think
        they've multiplied. Now I know they're not
a serious bother, nothing like finding,
        say, a clutch of classics scholars lurking
lunatic behind the furnace, but lemurs
        (in the suburbs!) this must *mean* something.

I tried, of course, believing in them
        at first. Feeding them. Leaving the garbage
downstairs. But this just made them mad.
        Attempts at bonding, an utter cluster
fuck. So I was left, then, with leaving them
        alone…that, or prayer. Now I no
longer know what goes on down there. I'm sure

there's more, there's always more. But beyond
that, beyond the certainty of a cellar
              settling in to its own unsettling
circus, beyond the fear of small black hands
              prying their way up into this world,
I only know this: I have to keep them out.

SASQUATCH

It appears whole from the dark lumbering,
great with hair, skull crested, unkempt, the sharp
musk of must preceding it then lingering
long after it vanishes behind a deadfall
into the ulalaic leaf whisper beyond.

> *The Sherpas call it Mehta-Kangmi,*
> *the devil of the snow. Others know it*
> *as the Wild Man only. Of Sumatra,*
> *Mongolia, of the Malayan jungle.*
> *In the West it has collected other names.*

Pulling my skins closer, I set out after
it, spelunking my way through forest
as if the green pine were stalagmites,
the nettled canopy above, a weave
of emerald earth rib grown arch and grave.

> *Bukwas, Gilyuk, Selahtik, Ohma.*
> *The Mono Grande knows it, and Ecuador.*
> *The Caucasus, the Pamirs of Afghanistan,*
> *all the high places. Each forgotten grotto,*
> *unculled copse, each rocky seam left unmined.*

Somewhere near the tree line where air loss gives
way to scrub, the mountain's bald scree, close
to a coven of hawthorn clutched about
a cauldroned vale, I recover its tracks,
bits of fur, twigs bending themselves to fetish.

> *Teddy Roosevelt believed. And Albert*
> *Ostman who claimed abduction by a whole*
> *pride. Lumberjacks, housewives, all with tales.*
> *Roger Patterson even filmed it once in Bluff*
> *Creek. We all remember that fuzzy footage.*

At some point, the issue becomes one
of validity. Whether I'm following
something real or only reeling myself
along behind my own eroded
tracks. My feet are real. I know. They hurt.

Some have called it memory, the shadow
of return. Reminder of our shagged savannah
past, that wild purity which comes from sharing
blood with brute. Maybe. Or maybe poetry
means nothing to it. Paper, pulp. Ink, a dark berry.

Weeks later, unwashed and weary as the beast
I've long ceased to follow, I stumble upon just
the jutted edge of civilization where,
poised on a ridge overlooking all I left,
I shrug and turn and shamble back slowly into the fir.

THE OBLONG BOX

These are the letters she never sent,
yellowed and frayed, their corners bent.
This is the love spoon, a Celtic token.
He bought it in Wales. Its bowl is broken.
Here lies the map like a folded door
that opens up on a Swansea shore.

And next to these is the scarf he sent her,
Stewart plaid to stave off winter,
a tape with love songs, Seventies mix:
Sonny and Cher, the Carpenters, Styx.
Here too his letters she read and hid
as brittle as shells of katydid.
The phone calls, the e-mails, won't fit in this drawer.
But my heart…. Ah, that's what the pine is for.

THE EIGHT THOUSAND YEARS
BETWEEN US

I.

I turn to her in the darkness, her back
brittle I think with a distaste for mine
having turned, touch again what the spine
has held suspended for so long, brush
nape and neck of her, the down that's drizzled
here, spread, the way maple keys molt in rain.

She flinches from my touch, pulling her loose
pillow closer, naked, balling herself
up to that edge where once the dog would stand
licking faces already wet with love.
In the long dark I can barely make out
which shoulder still draws me most, falling away.

I want her, her mouth to find mine wanting
hers, wonder at how—now that I suspect
it won't—all lips seem lost in the simple
　　　　act of closing.

II.

The Chinchorro people of northern Chile
skinned their dead, rolling supple flesh down whole
like oiled body stockings, then, unhinging
everything human, parsed that skeletal
syntax, leaving each beached mandible
inarticulate, disconsolate, mute.

After the reassembly, the bracing
of soles with sticks, the packing of cavities
with clay, after every skull was split, caulked
with llama fur and sea urchin, after
skin was at last returned, sutured, lacquered
back with black manganese, the Chinchorro

maintained their dead for decades, held their hearts
intestate, took them into their homes, beds,
talked with them, held them, loved them like the lives
        they had become.

RINGS

about my life again. Wheels within
wheels. How my parents are back together,
but landlord, tenant. Not husband, wife. Stuck
together like deep-sea anglers, each grown large
in the other's eyes, parasitic. I'm thinking
of using the other name, seadevils, when the phone

—No, I know you know, but I'm going to go
sometime. No, I'm giving them to you
to give to them. I know. I know it won't be
easy, but someone has to split them up.
I trust you, Babysan. I wouldn't ask
if I didn't know you didn't want

rings. Mother again. Division of property.
Should that be the theme? How we live
divided lives, caught between that deep
we never speak and— No, I almost spoke
of this to my class today and the moment
I began, all I could remember was my dad

—Don't you remember? She told the judge
I'd never given her anything. Used that
lie to squeeze me dry. That's when I took
the whole freezer-bagful up to his bench,
slapped it down like a sack of glass. This,
I said. This is the nothing I never gave her.

ringing me up and reaming me out again
over shit that happened twenty-five years
gone. How am I supposed to explain
to an audience that hasn't lived through it
what it does to a kid—and my class is
mostly kids—what it did to, say, my sister?

—You think I'm drunk. You think I'm drunk and calling
because.... You think I'm drunk don't you. Daddy
always thinks drunk when I call. But he doesn't love
anything not enough to not just buy stuff
remember the rings drinking Mother calling
our second dad Dad? He's dead, my real dead.

It's not like she calls all the time. In fact
it's been some time since the last booze breeze,
what Vonnegut calls a disease involving
alcohol and the telephone. Again
with the symbiosis. Like old memories.
How they circle back, follow us the way

October light strikes the wheels of the bike,
blows back like solar flack onto the cracked black
macadam where reflections resolve into small
suns, sundogs, rainbow rings that follow
me all the way from my house, up Dead Man's Hill
and on to Valhalla, the corner Redbud.

rings follow fingers around to palms
that put them on. I get calls. I try to tune
them out, screen for the folks, for my sisters
as easily as I do Chloe the Jamaican
Psychic, but there *are* those rings, late-night
baleful things, you know you can't escape. I

—don't know where she gets it, your sister.
Used to steal bottles from other kids at church.
Never let us hold her, saying, "Now, now...that's enough."
Last week your daddy bought your other *niece*
a doll for her birthday. All Cheri could say was,
"What about me? What about my *daughter?"*

don't want to hear her, my mom, talk Cheri
ever again. Or my dad blunder, even one more
time, around the pillar that is my mother.

But then, what else do they have? Mother—
expensive, multicolored diamonds notwithstanding—
works at Wal-Mart. My dad, retired, is full of

—Bullshit. I did try. Remember your senior year?
When I got them back, let you try and sell them?
Must have been forty-thousand-dollars worth
if they were a dime. No, I know it wasn't
that expensive. But just the first semester?
And why East Coast? You did just fine here.

regret. Regret and wrath and recrimination.
Big three or big W.... For her it's always
been *wallet*. Him? *Wife*. And neither can
stand the other, at least not as they are. Me?
All I wanted back in school was out. Wanted
fame, wanted everything in Oklahoma but

—the bleeding. I'm not afraid of after, just
the blood part. No not drunk. You have classes
tomorrow? How long till you grad— I know
it's a lot late but Daddy hung up on you
understand I'm not drinking not.... No, no knife.
Just scissors. How should I start? Wrists or the rest?

what it was. My sisters, pretty much the same.
They just found other dressings for their wounds.
If I write *my family was a string virus, crashing,*
bleeding out, would that be too much? Should I
just say, rather, *ring virus*? Play off puns again,
hide the seriousness behind the words, behind a

Bike left leaning on the storefront, silver
against glass, its handle-rack packed with books—
Fellowship of the Ring, *White Gold Wielder—*
I wander in, down magic rows of paperbacks
and magazines, past Famous Monsters,
Ringworld, *Lovecraft,* The Circle of Light

series of images I'm only just beginning
to craft from suffering? My mentor, Scott,
once told me you've only got three or four of these
before you go to hell. But this isn't exploitation.
Honest. It's the same as my sisters. One eloped
with God; another, exotic dancing; the youngest,

—might be different if she'd gotten married.
Okay, Beverly's didn't turn out, but still....
Remember how you were her ring bearer?
And her friend's, and your cousin's? Was it just
three times? So cute in that suit, those little boots.
You couldn't even say it. Called yourself "ring burier."

whatever wasn't likely. She turned to wine
only after. Which, were I really writing this poem,
would make me want riff off transubstantiation.
But this isn't poetry. Most of it probably
isn't even true. Seems I'm going to hell
anyway. At least that's what I imagine

—Little Bit called again, this time from their balcony:
"Mom's putting stuff up her nose." You should have seen
the bottles. Stopped counting at 99. No, they're fine. Wine
rings everywhere. No food in the house. Claims
her dad can't come, says he's dead. So, I try a doll,
but she won't leave the ledge, promises....

my dad will think if he ever reads this. It's not
like he doesn't love. Look again at that last
stanza. He *does* care. And it's not like
he beat us or locked us in some basement. Yet
how do you write *lack*? He lacks. Lacks what? Real
compassion? Maybe not that either. Daddy

—drove all over that summer in OKC you me
and the treehouse cousin Hal built the smell
of cedar now he's dead haunted houses

we made from entrails witch fingers the tent
in the backyard where we all played frog prince
blindfolded pretending to marry kissing our magic

drives us all nuts. And I don't know if we hate
the fact that he only knows how to buy us off,
or the fact that we need to know he'll be there
to buy us when we need it. Like Mother's
rings. I was only seventeen. I didn't know
how to sell diamond property. I didn't know

In back, beside boxes of wax lips and rubber
hearts, suction-cup horns, black lights, cardboard
boneyards, eyeballs in egg crates, just past racks
of records that advertise REAL SCREAMS
and RATTLING CHAINS, lines of monster rings
yawn across the shelves. Mummy, zombie, beast.

exactly what I wanted. I'd only ever sold shoes.
Read a lot. Wanted to write stories, like Tolkien.
One ring to rule them all, one ring to.... To tell
the tale of the Ring Bearer who braved the deeps
of Orodruin, braved demons, despair, doom itself
not to *find* treasure, no. To destroy one.

—rings. Just rings. There's enough to go around. Three
each, mostly. Red, green, blue. I trust you. Otherwise,
I'd just have to leave them on and let them bury—

Mother. She's just called again. Still wants
me to be her executor.... Do I let that one lie?
Could I execute her, her rings, her dark Lord?
Do I even try to write this? She's still
on the phone, at least in my head, still anything
but still, obsession wringing these words from

Each ring, a tiny plastic head, all mouth, all
agape. Drawn to them, to how my fingers find
and fill them, I feed their yaws, their toothy, open
Os as if they ache only for the immediate.
Standing in the Redbud, I watch my hands
accumulate open mouths, small skulls stuffed with

extremity, me, bringing back the most mundane
of memories. Nothing as grand as the Ring
Bearer's journey. No lurker in the dark, no
crack of doom. And I still don't know what keeps
us together, what always seems missing, why
I find myself writing

LUMINOUS BODIES

*But now I have come to believe that the whole world
is an enigma, a harmless enigma that is made terrible
by our own mad attempt to interpret it as though it had
an underlying truth.*
                    —Umberto Eco

AREA 51

Hush now. Take my hand. It's here, only just
ahead in this dry dark, the abandoned
dusk. Should you stumble, disturb the unseen
wires surely laid to stay our certain if
untimely arrival, should the moon be
overtaken by shadows of, say, silent
helicopters we may only imagine
exist, should strange, shifty men in long coats
black as the hearts we barely believe still
beat beneath them take us prisoner...squeeze.

You must remember I'm still here. Forget
nothing that you see. Take pictures. Keep notes.
If we *are* discovered, swallow the best
evidence. Cram the rest, whatever fits
into any orifice not too tight
with trembling to accept it. Where we are
going has no name—you won't devise it
on any map. This is a country within
a country, too improbable to remain
undiscovered long. Here, I have an extra

flashlight, gun, two canasta decks, a back
pack full of crumbs. The gate, should it appear
before us, won't be of much use. I hope
you haven't forgotten how to climb. No,
nothing toward the interior will be
easy—not the approach, not the casing,
not our final entry. Imagine
a warehouse full to the brim with mad
scientist stuff: tubs of acid, liquid
hydrogen, tesla coils alive with light....

More than likely there will be nothing
like this. Perhaps long tables, plastic bags,

rows of coroner's trays, a walk-in freezer.
We will fear whatever we find, because
what we find, I assure you, will be mundane.
Then, in one corner, behind some old ration
crates, maybe even packed inside, maybe—
remember, this is only our imagining—
maybe at last we will stumble on them,
our bodies, what we've come so far to see.

Do not touch. Stop breathing. Stop everything,
even the urge, suddenly, to evacuate.
Stay still, take it in the way you would a long
delayed dinner. Savor the distance, or, lacking
this, its opposite. No matter which, learn
to love what you now feel between yourself
and what lies before you. These, too, were travelers.
Look into those large eyes. Dare yourself to
distinguish there anything less than your own
story. This is what we were before coming

here. Alone.

RECOVERING ROSWELL

I.

Imagine for a moment it's all true:
You come upon four bodies in the desert
scree. Willow-thin, hairless as children,
scattered as if forgotten by their craft,

they collect your approach in dying
doe eyes. Offering the ones left living
water, you tug sheepishly at their seeming
weightlessness of limb, drag them some little

distance from the wreckage. One of them stirs,
captures your sleeve in its reedy fingers,
pulls you close to skin translucent as its eyes
could never be, opens what you believe

to be a mouth. What it tells you will change
everything. Now, imagine what must attend.

II.

A man comes home from a day worn blue,
dusty hair, raw hands, lines that make a hazard
of his face. His wife holds him, unbidden,
and he cries. She knows him, knows the heft

of his cares, sees something has shifted, lying
closer to the skin. How to explain grieving?
How, since to survive he must claim dreaming,
must believe nothing, must forget. The kettle

whistles for her. She goes. He prefers
to stay at the window awhile. Day lingers
between the beams only so long as the lies
last, fading, graying, counting on reprieve.

In the dark, near a crater, dry grasses arrange
a weedy requiem. Three movements. Three graves. Wind.

KEEP WATCHING THE SKIES

Over four billion years of Grace, and then what?
In the heart of the Yucatán, its deep
crater, down below the boundary between
thunder lizard and thunder god, between
the laying down

of one discarded mantle and another,
there is that which we will never recover,
that which set our planet reeling like a bell.
In the year 66, Josephus described a sword
hung over Jerusalem.

June twenty-fifth, Twelfth Century, five monks
watch the moon's upper horn split in two, spout
flame. And Moctezuma, and Giotto....
The end of empires, the beginnings of kingdoms,
heavenly ones, on Earth.

Harbingers. Heartbreak. A Siberian fireball.
Dead trees, dead dinosaurs, dead Tunguskan air.
From Chicxulub to Arizona, from a walled,
crater-carved city in Europe—its church
heat-flashed diamond—

back to the cold accumulation of Oort
itself, the sky is always falling. Somewhere. Great,
black, gap-toothed chunks of celestial snow, doom's
detritus cast down like Thrones from the walls
of heaven, or.... No.

The heart aches for so much more than just some rock,
haphazard, rent from the unremarkable
orbit it has always known. But stones, simple
stones are inevitable. Reason in collision, oblivion....
The heart's conceit.

WHEN WORLDS COLLIDE

After Mark Strand

I met her bolting vodka.
She was a lesbian.
We began by talking Wicca
and ended with Quaran.

I wouldn't remember the party,
whose house, whose porch, whose pot,
but she.... Now there was someone
best left not forgot.

Oh where does love descend from?
Does the Goddess really care?
Can a lesbian love a poet?
Do poets have a prayer?

She wore a hat of curtains,
a motley, wild chapeau,
and as we talked of scholarship,
abortion, Bush, Rimbaud,

her eyes beneath the drooping bill
began, like stars, to breathe,
cut loose from vast gas columns
in a stellar nursery.

Oh whom do we descend from?
Do bonobos do this dance?
When a tapir falls for an aardvark,
do they learn to share their ants?

I hadn't come to find this life,
nor she to alter hers.

Two Pecos-ridden twisters,
two pairs of magic spurs.

We spoke of what her goals were,
the anthropology
of Inuit and !Kung and Thai,
of dancing Balinese.

Does what we do in the daytime
mean squat when the bedsprings bend?
Does sex play even a role at all
in finding one's ampersand?

I told her I was just a year
from having the Ph.D.
She told me I could go fuck myself.
We both laughed mightily.

She was poor and she was stuck
in this one-horse college town;
no graduate programs to speak of,
no job, no cap, no gown.

Mere mortals, we are chattel
to space-time as it bends.
We let it ride, our hoary hides,
till Einstein's dice descend.

Her brain had been so famished
these last two years for learning.
But now she felt the gerbil had died,
the wheel still madly turning.

She told me where she worked part-time,
a card shop on the Square.
She told me three more times that night
as if it were a dare.

Oh where does love descend from?
Does the Goddess really care?
Can a lesbian love a poet?
Do poets have a prayer?

That night as I drove my Rabbit home
(some time 'round three o'clock),
I didn't yet know the rain had slowed,
the Ark had found its rock.

I wondered how she saw me,
shorthaired, overweight.
But when at last I tracked her down
she asked me for a date.

Do gender or predisposition
mean squat when the arrows fly?
Does Cupid wear a blindfold?
Can he put out his own eye?

The music was a polka band.
They played a hurdy-gurdy.
Our lovers sparked on the courthouse lawn,
no fears of getting dirty.

All of that came later:
sex, sweat, marriage vows.
Two cats, two dogs, two open minds,
two dildos to arouse.

This *is where love descends from.*
The Goddess, yes, she cares.
Lesbians fall for poets.
Poets don't have a prayer.

Two by two we boarded *we,*
trading thees for thous,

trading roles, reversing poles,
magnetic, whirling Taos.

Two running brooks, two thousand books,
two penchants to carouse,
two set of reins, two Thomas Paines,
two little Chairman Maos.

Mere mortals rarely ponder
how random quarks collide.
Curses, vodka, baseball cards
can, like the Lord, provide.

MARS AND RUMORS OF MARS

It was luscious once, some would say a garden.
Water grown pink, fonts without wall or warden
coursed past fields of almandine, steppes of finest jasper.
Here, over beryl, sand like alabaster,
the rivers descended, hollowing slow rills
one swallow at a time. Beneath mantled hills,
faded, rose-pressed skies, beneath a mountain
of fire long dormant, somewhere plain, the stain
of green must have spread slowly, in fits
punctuated by ice. The brute matrix
of life, the earliest leviathans…. What surprise
they must have weathered when rudimentary eyes
at last understood the sky was falling.

And that rock, some other mother's child hauling
itself down out of darkness, perhaps struck them
as funny. Perhaps not. Maybe in some dim
fashion they worried how their own children—
cast out by collision, borne off into the forbidden
vacuum above—would fare in another
place, a distant blue world whose own dither
and din would descend, then, from *them*. Did they,
these hypothetical parents, keen, preen, pray?
Should we, knowing they are gone, have words to say?

Everything we thought we knew last Tuesday
ended when that rock gave up its ghosts.
Microbes they say, fossils from another world. With boasts
full of what vast sadness comes from each new dream,
we pledged to return home, unpack the rocks, trace the stream
back from Nod and kill some nodding angel, steal
his flaming sword. No, it won't be that surreal,
yet this is how Eden *always* ends, shining
so bright the rest grows dim, as if it were beginning.

FIVE MILLION YEARS TO EARTH

...and there is faintly coming in
Somewhere the vast beast-whistle of space.
　　　　　　—James Dickey

JHVH, the Tetragrammaton, inchoate, ineffable,
the unspeakable name. In English, it becomes Jehovah,
Yahweh, or often, simply, Lord. Imagine the power
of such absence, how we yield to it, trembling, as if before
the abyss, itch to scratch each lack with the unintelligible
vowel hatch of prayer. With any distance, this is how we are,
riding leviathan down the fathoms to our next best
understanding. That first homely hominid, lost at the lip
of some volcano, trapped between ice and the fire she feels,
the bloody crown of birth come upon her, inopportune,
necessary, calling her to cave. Every emptiness. What matter
is mostly made of.
　　　　　In families we name it love, lapse, perhaps
gap, grant it generations. As a child, all I knew was Mother's
parents didn't live together anymore. These days, Paw Paw's
just a vague memory of cleft and crag, face like a tractor
seat, more hole than heavy metal, but *then*.... I remember
touching those cracks, running my fingers along what was left
of his life, counting the cigarette stains on his fingers.
He taught me to whistle, smoke, how divorce wasn't part
of the Baptist vocabulary. They lived a whole hundred
yards from one another. He, in his trailer, leaving only once
a week for crackers, soup, beer. She, prisoner of proximity,
in the house where they'd raised seven kids. He had his visions. She,
her quilts. And when he finally stopped coming out, when they had to pry
him from those sheets he'd become a part of, when the diabetes
he'd fed took an arm, a leg, claimed the whole turquoise taint
of him, his children gathered on Maw Maw's porch to watch him slip
away. Mother went to pieces.

There is nothing quite so terror-ridden
as the blank spaces between. Gods, continents, people, the deep
satisfaction of letters on a page. All our dark spark then,
every inkling, each kiln-clay fire of lucidity must be born
in transit, between one unvaulted void and the next. In the middle,
though, the dark matters. Even in binary systems where stars
spin their stories into primordial mass, where one gaseous ghoul
sups eternal on the other—pink plasma columns locking the two
in vain, vampiric vacuum dance—the way they embrace
around that nothingness they share indicates, well, the end
product. Progeny. Planets. Hope for what new knowing may come
across such gulfs.
      My father's folks suffered much the same. Grandma
died with the birth of my youngest aunt. So Grandpa and his hired hands—
Elvis, Ocie, their children, his—all moved in together. There was talk,
of course, when Elvis died, when they stayed together even then.
But they never split. When the children, my dad among them,
had long gone, still they found a house together in the city.
He held off in the top floor, she, in a bedroom near the basement.
And while the town died, as Grandpa began to remember
everything that had never happened—swimming the Rio Grande,
losing a leg in the field, sleeping with twelve curious cousins
all at once—as he forgot even Ocie, me, my father, curling
up into a ball they'd have to break his legs to get him out of,
close the coffin, he and his helpmeet refused to give ground.
All his life Grandpa denied that cellar. Each time tornadoes came,
he'd wander out into the lawn, watch them touch the land, recall
how he and Grandma stared them down.
      The destruction of the temple,
rending the curtain, bank foreclosure, your first lost lust.... All things,
even words, contain their dour doppelgänger. Black, once
blanc. Awful, full of awe. To reveal, replacement of the veil.
And yet still we remain, colored as if by collaboration.
In Patagonia, the people believe they're haunted, hunted
by a sect of male witches. The Brujería, the Committee,
Council of the Cave. They seek only sadism, saturnalia,
claim corruption a catechism. Members must scourge themselves
clean of baptism by forty days in a waterfall, kill

a best friend, exhume a Christian corpse and skin its breast, wear
the flesh each evening. A human waistcoat fresh with grease
and phosphorescence.
    In my father's house, there are no mansions,
only rooms. One for him, one for my mother, one for us.
It's strange, coming here again, as if to some sort of redemption.
They divorced when I was ten. And between then and now, between
three other husbands, two marriages, a girlfriend or four,
they've managed to return to this, unmarried, unhappy, quiet
but for the times the family reconvenes. And lying here
with *her*, knowing she too may leave, witness to that desire
I cannot help but envy, understanding the yaw she needs
to fill with further learning, I struggle with what comfort
even infants know, confronted with the strangeness of a face,
what our forebears must have prayed for in the Moon, what Schiaparelli
and Lowell molded out of Mars. Connections, canals, imagined
civilization. I linger on the lines between. Ionized
gas, Doppler-dazzled byways, connect the some hundred billion
galaxies we see. It is this, remnant of our ancestors' sea
years, a finger-fretted webwork I lace with mine that weds me
to her own as we lie here, grasping, dark.
    The Brujería
make children into monsters, disarticulate their limbs, stuff whole
left arms into oblivion, an incision in the chest. Then, inch
by inch they tourniquet the toddler's head till it turns back
upon itself, its gaze gracious with this gift, an uncorrupted view
now down the spine. They call it the *Invunche*, immobile,
immaculate, empty. Guardian of our entry to the cave.

THE SLAVE TRADERS OF GOR

As summer drew down, mosquito laden,
mayfly bound, each day translucent as that
wax paper they used to wrap Black Cat sparklers
in, each hour only half chalked, flocked with gunpowder
or grasshopper tobacco, twilight would find
us picking through horse pens where we played Ghost
In the Graveyard, taking each sweet turn in the "grave,"
or in my aunt's barn where rubber eyeballs
slathered in molasses stood stead for greater
terrors. My sisters and I lay luminous
those nights, two to a bed in Grandma's back
room, too hot to sleep easily, listening
to the sound of the air cooler chewing
luna moths to fine mist, and sometimes our hands
found one another in the dark under
the nubbed expanse of faded old throws,
imagining all we could of this world,
what it was we might of another. Other
days, picked scarce of horny toads or hand-lathed
pecan ray guns, sisters gone riding, my cousins
and I would find ourselves back in that same
back room, holed up with, at best, second-hand love
stories, all copped from older siblings, songs
from *Grease* playing on the eight-track, the notion
of family so distant as to be only
a kind of background radiation. Even then,
at ten, when tickling turned earnest and the kissing
began, I must have known I believed it
more than just a game. As their bright, brief mouths
suckled my own, bird hands swallowing
their way to the small of my spine, as they trussed
me up and tortured me, playing at being
something I suppose they already were—woman,
alien, and me their trusting slave—as I came to
understand how I understood absolutely

nothing of what I felt, I remember turning
every time to the juncture where that cot
kissed the wall, turning my back on what wanted
me, on what I wanted, as if by turning
I could wrest from them my own longing. Later,
we would all lie sweating, immanent, nearly
human again, save perhaps for one small face
still turned, forever turned, axis set on solstice.

THE BIRDS

Black flack. Croak and cackle racket. So the crows
are back, hundreds of them worrying the sky's purple
veins with their feet. Chinquapin and honey
locust, exposed, bare, sag beneath this unexpected
airborne swag as branches, brittle with November's
cold ennui, shatter like safety glass, echoing
in sound the sight their broken trellising
makes of a sky topped off with beating,
onyx bird breath, the puffing and showboating
all ravens do as they muscle this or that slim limb
into shape. It is time, they know, for new berths
somewhere up from the clutter of the day's dun
leaves.
       And as we stand on the porch watching
them I recognize their clotted forms, as yet
unfashioned fletchings, droppings, the chaos
each unruly bluster or boisterous black explosion
leaves behind. This whole tableau resolves then
into the branching brain it is. Nerve, neuron, sap,
synapse. All backlit, thrown into high relief.
And I see thoughts lighting, bursting into feather,
settling in, growing cold or warm, dim
or deft, more precisely piqued.
               I imagine
the trees imagining us and there, suddenly,
we are. Up.... No. Just.... Yes, there. Two ungainly
rooks, almost spontaneous, a bit bedraggled
but still perhaps believable. As if these great
dark boughs spreading, brooding here between us
and the setting sun have only this moment
begun to understand their need for us to be.

MISSION CONTROL

Weak signals may have been heard today
from the missing Mars Polar Lander....
                    —AP Wire Service

Come in.... Come back.
Please respond.... Come back.

Nothing but the crack of keys, an echo
in a cold room, your own voice lost between
here, where you are, and Mars. How far you've come
for this to be the end. It's as if a million-
plus miles were nothing now. Still, you knew
the risk from the beginning. One doesn't
set out to build bridges between such bodies
blind. So many catastrophes loom, always
possible, when what you're really doing
is falling. Burn up, burn out, controlled descent
into something unforeseen, a soft spot
perhaps, a rocky way, the occasional
crevasse. Loss of communication.

Come in.... Come back.
Are you damaged...? Come back.

Two bodies. Heavenly. Spheres that couldn't be
more different. And so you reach, totter
trembling into the unknown only to find,
finally, yourself in a mirror too red
to really see. You, not you. Origin
and end of all you are. A mixture then
of cairn and chemistry, propulsion and, well,
poetry. The hope some slick enigma attends
the other side. But now, alone in this place,
mission muddled, control all but gone, still

you sit and wait and toss echoes down the void
because you love even the thought of loss, this,
the abyss that exists only for having tried.

Come in…. Come back.
What else is heaven for?

WAITING ON THE BRASS BAND

They're coming today (tomorrow, outside)
with bright tasseled hats, trombone slide,
with sousaphone and cymbaled knees,
the sounds of arrival on borrowed breeze.

We dream of what songs, what instruments.
Fireworks. Colorful tents.
Hot dogs, smoke bombs, baseball, oboes,
processional, ballad, banjo solos.

We've needed them now for days, months, years.
We've run out of cheese for the celery spears,
the crepe paper's bleeding, torn down in spots,
we've lost the seller of tequila shots.

He married the girl who made paper birds.
They left when the sign-maker ran out of words.
Newspapers sleet down the street where blockades
once kept the traffic and penny arcades

from stumbling together, but now where we wait,
we see only taxis, an orange crate,
a bag lady preaching the band won't come.
But I tell you I hear them. Fife. Drum.

We've all been milling around, agape,
for so long now the ticker tape
has claimed our clothes where orioles nest.
Still decked out in Sunday best,

still agog, still here waiting.
The bag lady's screaming, masturbating.
Our pockets are filled with pebbles, rocks.
The town's overgrown with hollyhocks.

Our hands have grown to fit these stones.
So practiced are we in welcome.

AMERICAN GOTHIC

For Beauty's nothing
but beginning of Terror we're still just able to bear,
and why we adore it so is because it serenely
disdains to destroy us.
                    —Rainer Maria Rilke

AMERICAN GOTHIC

> And suddenly I find something, hiding
> down some hall in my head, though not
> my head but a *house*...
> —Mark Z. Danielewski

Sometimes it lurks just inside
the threshold, a formless figure
darker than the ink it inhabits
leaning on the yaw that is
your door. Other nights you hear it
in other rooms: the kitchen,
sweeping dead skin into wicker
baskets; the mud room, setting bones
in precise piles; the basement,
methodically knocking.

As long as you can remember
it's been there, waiting at the edge
of each sleep's door, in every house,
every city, guardian
at the lid to oblivion,
last ectoplast you see at night,
the black within black that harbors,
you suspect, a deeper darkness.
And though you've never seen them, you
imagine teeth too, row upon row.

All canine, no cuspids, the teeth
accordion like Lon Chaney's
in London After Midnight, *the blind*
crone's in House on Haunted Hill.
They say we control what haunts us,
what we raise from these Boggy Creeks
called hearts, but tonight you know it

will be there again, bloodless,
batlike, elbow walking its way
to the hem of your bed.

~ ~ ~

My father's first house had three rooms.
Bath, dining, living.... These don't count.
It's the bedrooms life lingers in.
Here, where we pile up simply
all we've ever had, everything
we'll never need. Partridge Family
albums, pennies in plastic buckets,
Bomba the Jungle Boy, photographs
of sink baths, old ledgers, old bills....
Whatever we have to remember.

My room was filled with schooners,
tiny ships my father ferried back
from across seas he'd only skimmed
in DC-10s. A dragon-prowed
Viking vessel. A Vietnamese
sloop tooled in teak. From Thailand,
two metal yawls. A Peruvian straw
junk that wouldn't stay bound.
And then my favorite, a ketch, all
shells, even its sails, from Tai pei.

My sisters' room was crowded too.
A whole wall of dolls, homunculi
from Hawaii, Spain, Japan, the litter
of various lands. Ice, Green, Newfound.
Some dressed, some nude, a few whose heads
opened into odd, whole-body purses,
but each color coordinated.
Purple equaled eldest, green, youngest,
red, right in the middle. From room
to room we wandered through the world.

～～～

Black-spatted vampire, cataract-
wracked witch, night itch.... It could be
anything, nothing, all Lovecraft
ever dreamed. In "The Dreams in the Witch
House," he tells us he's heard "the wild
whispers of the chimney-corner,"
explains how even THE three evil books
don't loosen cobbles between us
and "them" as easily as, say, odd
angles, numbers, a house's history.

Dickens was right. Ghosts come in three
flavors: what you despise, yet cannot
escape; what you are and don't wish
to be; what you crave, but cannot have.
Professional ghost hunters remain
torn. Some indeed say three, others, two,
and though folklorists make it worse,
by the thousands, haunting is simple,
like Christmas. The past. The future.
Divided by impossible presence.

The Field Guide to Ghosts *breaks*
them down into Revenants,
Apparitions, and Harbingers,
some crisis, some non, some simply time
slips. The Ghost Hunter's Bible *posits*
poltergeists are linked to human agents—
women, usually—who tick on,
hugger-mugger, like Typhoid Mary.
Anxiety, obsession, any emotional
tension sets the tables turning.

～～～

And our parents? Their room always
seemed mostly Mother's. Hearts blown
from carnival glass, a whole family
of porcelain mice, two hundred pairs
of shoes. On the walls, paintings
by my dead cousin, a Japanese
print of Mt. Fugi in winter,
a shadow box—one angel per
month. A bell beside the bed, a glass
of ice water, pills. Then, of course, her.

On the front door hung a plaque.
THE DIETRICHS written in mock
Japanese characters, the Ts
and Hs tapered like miniature
pagodas. Six figures, Weeble-ish
bubble people, wobbled beneath
the name in colored kimonos.
Black and white for my folks. Purple,
red, green for my sisters. Blue for me.
Round. All of us. Perfect and impervious.

Under this, a peephole bored
through the door. On summer days,
around six, the sun shone through
that tiny glass and cast a dot,
rainbow shot, on the opposite
wall, lighting another plaque inside.
In the corner behind Mother's
rocker, it read, "For God so loved
the world...." Each August day
we would line up, let that light mark us.

~ ~ ~

From Fate *magazine, 1959:*
"Although I seemed to be asleep
I suddenly felt a heavy pressure

on my body. There were two of me
and one of me had its eyes open
and could see. The other one of me
felt pressure and was trying desperately
to open its eyes and rid itself
of what seemed a horrible crushing
nightmare." Incubi, succubi....

Some say the gods have given up
their ghosts. Recent REM research
suggests we who half wake during dreams—
arms and legs anesthetized by nature,
by the body's own stopgap to stop sleep-
walking—we fill in futility, that fear,
with our best, most recent bogeys.
It's what we've always done. What holds us
down, what's now little grey men, was once
lamiai, Lilith, langsuyar. Wampir and witch.

One night, unable to sleep, Lord
Dufferin goes to the window, sees
a man bearing a long box on his back.
The man turns, looks at the Lord.
Their eyes meet, Dufferin shudders
and he recognizes his casket. Years
later, in Paris, he sees the man again,
approaching an elevator. He steps
back, shocked, as the lift doors close,
the cable snaps, and everybody dies.

~ ~ ~

In the evenings my sisters cooked,
usually potpies, Spam. Sometimes
we went out. Tuesdays were Sirloin
Stockade night. I loved the bull
that stood like Bunyan's blue ox
on rollers outside. Some nights Mother

came with us. Mostly not. *That*
Stockade isn't anymore. In '78,
before they were shot, six people
were locked in the freezer there.

During the afternoons, each taking
turns keeping Mother's water filled,
we played Twister, Which Witch is Witch,
Old Maid, Who Stole the Diamonds?.
Or, more often than not, watched TV.
I remember *Genie* and *Bewitched*,
The Flying Nun, so many strong,
powerless women. And Daddy?
Barring Tuesdays, he was off—France,
the Azores—bringing back our colors.

Some summers they dropped us off
at Maw Maw's or Aunt Arleda's.
Other times we'd head to Six Flags.
The last time Mother summered with us,
rain made my father mad. Spent
the whole day on an Arctic raft.
The final trip of *any* kind we took
together was when we packed up
everything and headed to Lockney
for a week, another aunt's house.

~ ~ ~

"When any particular organized
system ceases to exist…its organizing
field disappears from that place.
But in another sense, morphic fields
do not disappear: they are potential
organizing patterns of influence,
and can appear again physically
in other times and places…they contain

*within themselves a memory
of their previous physical existences."*

As such, The Presence of the Past
*doesn't tell us anything we shouldn't
already know. What we do remains.
Wherever we do it resonates.
You've often wondered what happens
to Schrödinger's cats, which one—it
or its twin, both trapped in six-sided
boxes—is living or dead, knowing
full well that if no one feeds them, both
will be both dead and alive, forever.*

*Fetch, ka, bean sidhe, doppelgänger.
Whatever the real ones are, whether
you believe in haunted houses or no,
no matter if the thing at the foot
of the bed is you or someone else, dead
child, dead parent, mysterious
morphic field, toenails in moonlight....
No matter if it's matter, gone, gray,
you still love to haunt the haunted
even if you have to pay.*

~ ~ ~

A fight—more father froth, Ross wrath—
made him turn around the minute
we arrived. Six hours back home,
at midnight. Though the next day
they were reconciled, though we did
return in the end, it was Mother
who seemed to stay behind. Even later,
when it was just the girls, Daddy, me,
before I was old enough for haunted
houses, the scares had to come in bites.

So, Lion Country Safari, Seven
Seas, The Gun Fighter's Hall of Fame.
Once, at the latter, wandering
around a display of a late night
lynching, past signs that said NOT
FOR CHILDREN, the whole thing
boarded up like an abandoned mine,
I peeped through the lowest knothole
and saw six would-be Bill Bonneys
dancing from the ceiling in shadows.

I never told anyone what I'd seen,
how the heads were almost off on two,
blood everywhere. Later that week,
on a ride called the Monster, maybe
the Tarantula, suspended between
tarmac and terror, head spinning,
the world walking away, I imagined
how it must have been for them.
I saw my cousin collapsing in sand.
I saw Mother ringing her bell.

~ ~ ~

Unliving room, master deadroom
endless hallway. Faux graveyard,
vortex tunnel. There are books,
whole shelves of haunted self-help.
HOW TO MAKE YOUR OWN rotting
flesh. Papier-mâché tombstones right
beside duct-tape bodies. G: glow in the dark
pigment powder. H: head on a table.
O: oscillating werewolf fan. S: skull
nightlight, or spooky, subset: Tree.

A through Z. Animatronic
to zombie. Every haunted house
has to have them: pneumatic corpse

and neck stump, self-rocking chair
and asynchronous flickering lamp.
What hovers: dangling crank spider,
hanging skeleton cage. What emerges:
pond monster, Peter Pumpkinhead.
What disturbs: blood transfusion
bottles, punch-bowl baby doll.

Forget the jack-o-lanterns, the sheets,
bobbing for fruit like a cute cadaver.
To make a melting skull you will need
one styrofoam head, about ½
pound of paraffin, one pot, a cookie
sheet, spoon, paintbrush, crayolas.
Add paint, masking tape and Christmas
lights. Or if you wish to cobble,
say, a standard wooden coffin,
directions can be found below.*

~ ~ ~

One Christmas, all my dad wanted
was three words. Little ones he said.
And it would be maudlin if it weren't
true. An act of language. A verb, two
pronouns. But as I hunkered under
the tinny rustling of our aluminum
tree, under red balls bathed in the tri-
colored fracture of manufactured
light spinning the tree turquoise,
magenta, stoplight orange....

As I clutched each treasure up
from beneath our melted angel
perching drunk among the topmost
branches, wand and arm gone limp,
I didn't find schwas or labials,
no voiceless interdentals,

only big red Xs, no *mas*.
My father gave her all he had
to give that year. Another ring.
Another cold circle of light.

And she took it, added it
to the others already growing
heavy on her hands, as if she were
that tree itself, adding rings with each
year, oblivious to all those old
saws that promised to bring her down,
woodman with her, unaware
of how far she had come from that
seventeen-year-old hanging bedsheets
over blinds over windows.

~ ~ ~

Ever since you first heard "The Man
With the Golden Arm," the first time
you watched Dr. Phibes Rises Again
or at last recognized yourself
as stuck, sealed off in this body
we all have to ride to the grave....
You'd think by then you would have known
what terrors lay ahead, what gothic
bluster a summer of sister pester
and cousin cluster had prepared for you.

Yet approaching Aunt Arleda's
barn, its badly weathered wood whorl
lowing in the wind like a brinded
cow, Lee flares skirting devil's
claw and pumpkin gourd, barely
ten, lurching between a rusted
limbo lattice of what everyone
around Carnegie called "bob wire"

to reach the door, your stomach still
stuttered up larynx rung by rung.

Just inside the door, you had to pass
horse-blanket curtains hung haphazard
to mute the light, step, stumble, and enter
that ersatz haunted house the others
had made. It was your first. As you turned
the corner, set foot in the fear
factory proper, something approached,
a cowled figure darker than surrounding
shadow, a witch with teeth that glowed, blood
descending from her lowermost lip.

~ ~ ~

Each time, afraid. Each time watching
her husband leave. She who knew nothing
of sex. Even less of the man
who wooed her on the wing, whetted her
with the wail of jets. Now, four kids
and forty thousand dollars in debt....
I don't know if she ever told him
after that, returned what he thought
he had given. I just guessed
the words, aloud, like he wanted.

Before the first divorce, another
room had to be added, this one
outside, away, on the other side
of town. As far from the old house
as she from her hysterectomy.
Mother's new apartment, alive
with lava lamps and Godseyes, paved
in paisley and leopard print, spotted
from bath to boudoir like all the new
panties and bras he'd bought her.

Three years later I'm shoveling skivvies
into the washer at our *own* new
apartment when Fayoma, third
aunt of four, phones my dad to get even.
While I portion out parts of Tide
to dirty laundry, Daddy takes the call.
She reveals what went on in that room.
Dozens she says. Our doctor, probably
the preacher, a TV repairman. The night
tumbles away. Wash, rinse, repeat.

~ ~ ~

Her fingers clawed out to catch you
where you stood, frozen inside
the barn, behind its blind eyes, trapped
inside its mind, the Midwest, this red plain
you'd grown up in, believing it all.
Werewolves, witches who braid mare manes
at midnight. The story of "Lavender,"
Lugosi, Lanchester. You believed
in Price, in paradise, in your parents,
in everything coming after you.

Exhibit A: You and your siblings list
lost among tombstones, broken teeth
rising through fog. In the house, the first
room, a laboratory. The mad
staff, encephalitic, long-toothed elves.
A woman tied to a bloody gurney.
Hacksaw. Strobe. No anesthetic. The leg
comes off. As. She. Looks. Right through you.
Like your sister always did, chasing you
room to room, after you handed her the knife.

Exhibit B: You and your father prowl
the last passage where you know by now
a chainsaw has to be. Near a small stone

grove meant to pass as ossuary, the man
in the hockey mask leaps from behind
PVC and papier-mâché elm.
As the two of you bolt for the final
door, you fall. Crossing to the threshold,
your father crosses you, his terror
nearly tearing you in half.

~ ~ ~

"Whosoever shall put away his wife,
saving for the cause of fornication,
causeth her...." He *had* been saving.
He had bought. Apartment, clothes, second
marriage, three years.... But nobody knew
this then. Even the aunts just assumed
he'd had her committed. And me?
I had a new place to swim, a library
with *The House with a Clock in Its Walls*,
Bradbury's "The Man Upstairs."

1976. Year of independence.
The first divorce was a lot like second
grade. Back during the bed days—
Mother ringing her bell, Daddy off
to elsewhere—they sent me to preschool
every morning, real school only
after. When the final bell rang
I had to wait at the front of the school,
watch through vast, elementary
windows for a blue VW van.

Then Hillside Christian Daycare. More
waiting. The final leg. First day
of daycare I forgot, went to find
my mom at the school corner. An hour,
maybe more. Then to Mother's stylist,
her house across the street, tears. Finally

she came for me. I found it was less
than three blocks only *after* Mother
took custody, when I started walking
home. I never passed that way again.

~ ~ ~

Exhibit C: You and your best friend
arrive late at the haunted warehouse,
downtown OKC. The line's backed
up to where the Federal Building
soon will only once have been.
Discussing Poe and Du Maurier,
what Derleth did to his betters,
all the masters, old and new—
Jacobs, Jackson, Barker, Brite—
you move with the line, you enter.

Somewhere between abattoir
and exit you abandon your hope
to the labyrinth, give in to the heart's
vertigo, your eyes bootless, hands
begging braille from walls. As you turn yet
another blind corner, growing ever more
inverted, your fingers find it. It screams,
you both scream, the terror sudden,
but done. Now you have to consider
this kid, about ten, more lost even than you.

So, ghost, you wander through your houses.
Six walls, six homes and more between
you and the others, leaving a trail
of yourself behind, connecting
wall to wall to wall until the boxes
you've occupied connect and blur,
bleed out across both yaw and year.
Physicists, describing time, name this

hypercube. Like the spirit, it can't
exist. A door as real as you.

~ ~ ~

Not long after that first divorce,
awkwardly dating my dad again,
Mother made a trade. Lay for loot.
Rights for rings. Daddy got *me*
in the deal, half of what he wanted, while
Mother walked away with wampum.
The last night in our first house I woke
to see a familiar form lurking just inside
my door. I couldn't breathe. I swear
at the hospital I saw it once more.

Still, nothing, not even more marriages
set them free. Senior year. Two husbands,
six, maybe seven seasons later,
Mother, bruises yet brilliant
on her neck, jumped ship, left her trucker
terror behind and stayed a few months
with Daddy and me. It wasn't long
before my father's furies cast her
adrift again, his money running short,
tired of trial-size redemption.

Now it's going on six years. Mother
and Daddy together at last. Divorced,
yes, but still sharing towels. After
number three, my mom couldn't make it
alone. My dad even called to ask
what I thought. "I'm going to have
a boarder," he said. And I, "Just be
careful." To her, "Are you sure? You
know he still loves you." She, "I trust
it's only temporary."

~ ~ ~

See, the Gothic is not what scares us,
it's not what waits in grates, below
floorboards. It isn't what wails
across tarn or tunnels between
studs behind drywall. It doesn't live
even in stone, though stone, you might
suppose, is closer to the heart
of the matter. From Headlong Hall
to Harvest Home, Dorian to Denver,
each Gothic says the same. Stay, die.

But then we're all afraid of what lies
outside the fire. When the embers
gutter, when wind fans that old glow
and it wanders up and out of the pit
threatening, finally, the home
you've built around what was once
only warmth, when you find yourself
running from that light out into a dark
whose cold is less convivial, yes,
but also holds less terror than being....

What? Consumed by the sublime?
When the stars call down coldly, crow's
wing touches hair, and the knowledge
finally arrives that you are, indeed,
alone again, there must always come
an even greater terror, that of having
left the wrong dread behind. So,
primitive in your longing, tentative
and green, stained by your own mad thrust
into pine, you begin the trip back.

~ ~ ~

My father's house still has three rooms,
his and Mother's. Another to separate
the two. Over the front door hangs,
unfaded, the old DIETRICHS plaque.
Betty Boop and Precious Moments
(Mother's, all) cover every surface.
The old China cabinet stands again
in one corner of the kitchen, six
sheaves of dead roses interred on top.
Six more singles hang from the wall.

Today, his *new* room is just as mad
as mine once was, his walls barnacled
with jets he never flew, with the future
of ships, the fabled Enterprise
in over 300 incarnations. Beside
Tarzan, Thuvia, maid of Mars,
beside *White Fang* and all the Holmes
he never understood, one room over
from my mother...his *Trek* collection.
Everything he craves, but cannot have.

My mother's room reminds me
of my sisters'. Chock-a-block with dolls.
In here, it's always dark, door forever
closed. A towel at the entrance to keep
her smoke from escaping. More Precious
Moments, tiny green dragons, a chair where
she sits listening for what she despises
yet can't escape. Over the door,
another plaque. THE WITCH IS IN.
When all she wants is out.

~ ~ ~

*Here, even among only fragments,
you hope to find it. A broken branch,
a bit of bark laid bare, a footprint.*

Any token of yourself left behind.
Even back at the edge of the pit,
near the door still hanging open,
in the shadows where your house once
huddled too close to flame, between beams
that, now, lean on air alone, crossing
a foundation fatally wounded

~ ~ ~

you find, I find, my father
standing just outside the threshold
of my mother's door, formless,
a figure darker than the ink
he inhabits, arm raised as if
to knock. Inside, my mother
sits in her chair, what's left of her
life, smoking, blinds drawn, sheets
tacked to windows. Both afraid.
Both aware the knock will never come.

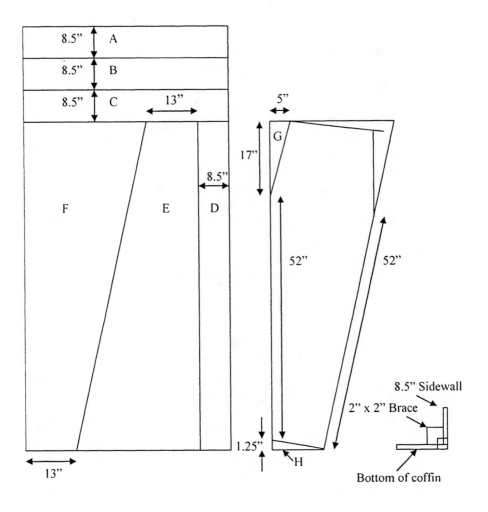

ARS POETICA

Start with the darkest corner of what was
the left ventricle. Twine will work, granted.
But waxed kite string or rusted piano
wire would serve better. You'll need a needle,
strong, curved, barbed and thick as a walrus'
penis bone. Begin by sewing it back
to back with its twin, the right ventricle.
This is where, perhaps, the trouble started,
where all that bad blood built up, returned
from limbs rather shaken now, pale, in need
of a pulse against which they used to rail.

Now you have the beginnings of something
useful. That teak pegboard you made for just
such an occasion— Hang your monstrosity
there while you consult the right auricle
for clues to continued reconstruction.
I suggest Krazy Glue, handy wipes, vast
reservoirs of patience. Soon you will have
to turn all four compartments inside out,
which is to say *right*side out, since they've been
wronged like removed rubber gloves already.

Before this, though, before the final suture,
there is much yet to consider. Septum....
Check. Pulmonary artery.... Check. Veins,
innominate and not, rushing semi-
lunar valve, aorta, assorted ducts....
Tape will work as well as roofing nails, and,
frankly, there are enough holes as is. There.
Now that you've spot-welded, warped, torqued your last
bolt, now that all which was venal begins
again to clarify, you need only
put it back. Call your witness. Add the current.

NOTES

The Mummy's Hand:

The hieroglyphic titles heading each of these sonnets come directly from the Egyptian Book of the Dead. They translate respectively as: "The Dead Body," "The Living," "Eternity," "My Heart, My Mother," "And They Fell Down," "The Keeper of My Head," "Eater of the Dead."

In the Valley of the Kings:

The *kua* (or trigrams) preceding each section of this poem come from the I Ching; I used only four of the possible eight. They translate: "Water," "Mountain," "Earth," "Heaven."

Bryan D. Dietrich lives in Wichita, Kansas with his new wife Gina and their son, Nick. Professor of English at Newman University, Bryan has won the *Paris Review* Prize, the "Discovery"/*The Nation* Award, a Writers at Work Fellowship, the *Isotope* Editor's Prize, and the Eve of St. Agnes Prize. A five-time finalist for the Yale Younger Poets Series, Bryan has been nominated for both the Pushcart and the Pulitzer. His poetry has appeared in *The Paris Review*, *Ploughshares*, *Prairie Schooner*, *The Harvard Review*, *The Yale Review*, *The Nation*, *Shenandoah*, *Weird Tales*, and many other journals. His first book, *Krypton Nights*, was published in 2002. Bryan grew up watching classic horror movies and is still conflicted about choosing a tenure-track job over a chance to be an extra in Tim Burton's *Mars Attacks*. He is, however, comforted by the fact that the first person abducted in *Aliens* is named Dietrich.

Printed in the United States
113256LV00003B/357/A